W9-CCN-615

The Irish couple walked into a bar. The wife looked around, then said to her husband, "You see that man downing one drink after another at the end of the bar? That's O'Malley, and he's been drinking like that since I jilted him ten years ago."

The husband said, "That's ridiculous. I don't care how good the reason, ten years is too long to celebrate."

*   *   *

Mrs. O'Brady was gossiping with a friend. "You know," she whispered, "I heard Colleen was pregnant when she was married. Is that true?"

"Well," Mrs. O'Sullivan replied, "they did throw puffed rice at her wedding."

*   *   *

A man knelt in the confessional and said, "Father, yesterday I got so mad that I went out and killed an Irish politician."

The priest said, "I don't care about your community service work. I'm here to listen to your sins."

*   *   *

Why did God create liquor?
So an Irishman wouldn't be Pope.

⊘ **SIGNET**   (0451)

RIB TICKLERS!

☐ **MAD VERTISING, or Up Madison Avenue, An Accumulation of Asinine and Atrocious Advertising Approaches by Dick DeBartolo and Bob Clarke.** You've been duped, taken, swindled, cheated, lied to, conned, and abused by advertising for years! But now, for the *first time*, you are being offered a *real chance* to save money by buying this book (which just might save your life)!   (067398—$1.25)

☐ **1,001 GREAT JOKES by Jeff Rovin.** Over 1,000 jokes, one-liners, riddles, quips and puns—for every audience and every occasion. Among the topics skewered in this collection are: bathrooms, yuppies, hillbillies, sex, small towns, weddings, writers and much more!   (168291—$4.95)

☐ **1,001 MORE GREAT JOKES by Jeff Rovin.** Once again we've set a new standard in the wittiest, wackiest, most outrageous in adult humor. Here are jokes for every occasion—from raising chuckles from friends and family, to rousing roars of laughter from all kinds of audiences. Even better, the jokes are organized alphabetically by subject—so open up this book for a nonstop feast of fun from A to Z.   (159799—$3.95)

☐ **500 GREAT JEWISH JOKES by Jay Allen.** How did they know Jesus was Jewish? Why did the Jewish mother have her ashes scattered in Bloomingdale's? What's a Jewish porno film? Find out the hilarious answers to these jokes and much more!!   (165853—$3.50)

Prices slightly higher in Canada

Buy them at your local bookstore or use this convenient coupon for ordering.

NEW AMERICAN LIBRARY
P.O. Box 999, Bergenfield, New Jersey 07621

Please send me the books I have checked above. I am enclosing $_____
(please add $1.00 to this order to cover postage and handling). Send check or money order—no cash or C.O.D.'s. Prices and numbers are subject to change without notice.

Name_____

Address_____

City _____ State _____ Zip Code _____
Allow 4-6 weeks for delivery.
This offer is subject to withdrawal without notice.

500 GREAT IRISH JOKES

BY
JAY ALLEN

A SIGNET BOOK

SIGNET
Published by the Penguin Group
Penguin Books USA Inc., 375 Hudson Street,
New York, New York 10014, U.S.A.
Penguin Books Ltd, 27 Wrights Lane,
London W8 5TZ, England
Penguin Books Australia Ltd, Ringwood,
Victoria, Australia
Penguin Books Canada Ltd, 2801 John Street,
Markham, Ontario, Canada L3R 1B4
Penguin Books (N.Z.) Ltd, 182-190 Wairau Road,
Auckland 10, New Zealand

Penguin Books Ltd, Registered Offices:
Harmondsworth, Middlesex, England

First published by Signet, an imprint of New American Library,
a division of Penguin Books USA Inc.

First Printing, February, 1991
10 9 8 7 6 5 4 3 2 1

Copyright © Jay Allen, 1991
All rights reserved

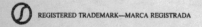
REGISTERED TRADEMARK—MARCA REGISTRADA

Printed in the United States of America

Without limiting the rights under copyright reserved above, no part of this publica-
tion may be reproduced, stored in or introduced into a retrieval system, or transmit-
ted, in any form, or by any means (electronic, mechanical, photocopying, recording,
or otherwise), without the prior written permission of both the copyright owner and
the above publisher of this book.

BOOKS ARE AVAILABLE AT QUANTITY DISCOUNTS WHEN USED TO PROMOTE PRODUCTS OR
SERVICES. FOR INFORMATION PLEASE WRITE TO PREMIUM MARKETING DIVISION, PENGUIN BOOKS
USA INC., 375 HUDSON STREET, NEW YORK, NEW YORK 10014.

For Bill, Val, and Marty,
whose home is always
filled with laughter.

CONTENTS

CHAPTER 1

GREAT IRISH JOKES
ABOUT DRINKING

Mickey O'Shannon was weaving his drunken way down the street one day when he ran into the priest. The priest admonished, "You ought to be ashamed of yourself. The more you drink, the smaller and smaller you make yourself, until you're more of a mouse than a man."

Frightened, O'Shannon made his way home. He stormed into the house, woke up his wife, and told her, "If you notice I'm starting to shrink, I want you to kill that blasted cat!"

How can you tell an Irishman in a topless bar? He's there to drink.

Why did God create liquor? So an Irishman wouldn't be Pope.

Did you hear about the Irish weight-lifting competition? The winner hoisted a forty-nine-ounce glass.

Why don't they cremate Irishmen? Last time they tried, it took a week to put out the fire.

An Irishman was staggering down the street when a lady said disapprovingly, "Every time I see you, you have a bottle in your hand!"

The Irishman burped, then replied, "Gee, lady, I can't keep it in my mouth all the time."

Why did the Irishman fill his swimming pool with beer?
He figured he couldn't drown, since the deeper he sunk, the higher he got.

What's the sexiest four letter word to an Irishman?
Beer.

Why is an Irish bar like a porno movie house?
They're both filled with a bunch of guys getting stiff.

The Irish judge returned from the pub one night so bombed that he threw up all over himself before he got upstairs. In the morning, he told his wife that a drunk had thrown up on him on the bus.

The judge made it to court, but during a recess he decided his story of the night before was not completely convincing. He called his wife and said, "You'll never guess what happened. That drunk who threw up on me was in court this morning, and I gave him thirty days."

His wife replied, "You better make that sixty days. He shat in your pants, too."

What's a "pick up" in an Irish singles bar?
A glass.

An Irishman took a sip of stout, then complained, "This stuff is horrible."

The pub keeper replied, "I don't know what you're complaining about. You've only got a pint. I've got thirty barrels of the stuff."

The drunk was standing in front of his house fumbling at the front door when his neighbor came out and asked, "Paddy, can I help you with that key?"

"Nah," the Irishman said. "I'll handle the key. You just keep the house from swaying."

The Irishman was sitting by the bedside of his dying friend. With his last breaths the friend looked up and said, "Paddy, I want you to do one thing to remember me. Every time you walk into our beloved pub, order a drink in my name." Then he closed his eyes and died.

Sure enough, Paddy kept his friend's memory. Every time he wet his whistle, he ordered one pint for himself and one for his dead friend.

One day, however, Paddy walked up to the bar and said, "Sean, give me one pint."

The bartender asked, "Paddy, I've never seen you order less than two at a time. Aren't you keeping your friend's memory?"

The offended Irishman said, "Of course I am. But the doctor's ordered *me* on the wagon."

The doctor examined the Irishman, then said, "I'm not positive what's causing those stomach pains. I think it's drinking."

"That's okay," the Irishman replied. "I'll come back when you're sober."

Did you hear about the Irishman who married the bootlegger's daughter?
He loves her still.

What's the definition of infinity?
The length of time necessary to form an Irish chapter of Alcoholics Anonymous.

Why does the Irishman keep a case of empty whiskey bottles in the basement?
For visitors that don't drink.

What's a queer Irishman?
A guy who likes women better than whiskey.

What do Irishmen take for a hangover?
Whiskey—the night before.

What's Irish Anonymous?
If you feel like going on the wagon, a couple of
drunks bring a bottle over.

What's a problem drinker in Ireland?
A guy who never buys.

What's an Irishman's favorite drink?
The next one.

Why do Irish women treat Irishmen like babies?
They have to have a bottle every three hours.

Did you hear about the Irishman who decided to
donate his body to science?
He also decided to preserve it in alcohol until he
died.

What's worse than drink to an Irishman?
Thirst.

Where does an Irishman go on vacation?
To a different bar.

What do you get when you cross an Irishman and a Jew?
A drunk who gets his liquor wholesale.

What's the Irish definition of reality?
An illusion produced by a severe alcohol deficiency.

An Irishman walked into a bar. The bartender told him, "We have a special today. All the beer you can drink for five dollars."

The Irishman said, "Great. I'll take ten dollars' worth."

How do you make an Irishman's tongue turn black?
Pour whiskey on a freshly tarred road.

The obviously inebriated Irishman staggered up to the hostess and asked, "Do lemons have tails?"

"What?"

"Do lemons have tails?" the drunk repeated.

"Of course not," the woman replied.

"Well, then," the drunk continued, "I'm afraid I have to tell you that I've just squeezed your canary into my vodka and tonic."

Why is an Irishman's second week in Alcoholics Anonymous easier than the first?
By the second week he's drinking again.

The Irishman at the bar had drunk so much that the bartender asked him to leave. The customer insisted he wasn't drunk, and he'd prove it. "See that cat coming in the door?" he said. "Well, that cat has only one eye, and that proves I'm not smashed."

"You're drunker than I thought," the bartender said. "That cat isn't coming in the door, he's going out."

What's the difference between an Irish pub keeper and a proctologist?
A proctologist only has to deal with one asshole at a time.

Two drunks were lying by the curb outside a bar when a cop came up. Recognizing one of the sots, the cop said, "Paddy McDougal, why do you have your finger up that guy's ass? That's sick."

"Oh, I'm not sick," Paddy protested. "It's my friend Sean that's sick. I'm trying to make him throw up."

"Well, how is sticking your finger up his ass going to make him throw up?"

"Just wait," Paddy said, "until I put it in his mouth."

O'Malley put away pint after pint, until he could barely stand. But the drink made him horny, too. He saw a woman sitting at the end of the bar, so he staggered over and slipped his hand down the rear of her slacks.

Furious, she turned around and demanded, "What do you think you're doing?"

"Sorry," he slurred. "I thought you were my wife."

"You're nothing but a stinking, stupid, drunken old sot," she shouted.

"Funny," O'Malley said, "you sound like my wife, too."

O'Malley and O'Toole staggered out of the bar, having struck out on their attempts to pick up women. They careened around a corner when in front of them loomed a mailbox and a fire alarm attached to a telephone pole.

O'Malley exclaimed, "Wow, look at those two broads."

O'Toole grumbled, "Forget it. The fat one in blue doesn't say a word, and the red one screams her head off if you touch her."

What happened when the Irish drunk saw the "Wet Paint" sign?
He did.

Why did the Irish guy have to take the freight elevator?
He always came home loaded.

Why was the Irish guy running around outside with his tongue out?
Someone told him there was a nip in the air.

Why did twenty-seven thousand Irishmen go north of the border?
They saw billboards that read, "Drink Canada Dry." So they decided to try.

The judge looked sternly down at the Irishman and said, "Plain and simple, it's alcohol that has brought you here before me a half-dozen times in the last two months."

Paddy replied, "Thank you, Your Honor. Everybody else was saying it was my fault."

What do you know about an Irishman that falls in the river?
It's the only water he's touched all day.

What's Irish rheumatism?
You get stiff in a joint.

How do you know an Irish patient is recovering? When he's well enough to blow the foam off his medicine.

O'Malley and O'Reilly were staggering home from the pub when the call of nature came. They were pissing when O'Malley said, "That's strange. When my water's coming out, it sounds like a waterfall up in the mountains. But when you pee, I don't hear a thing."

O'Reilly replied, "That's because you're pissing on the road. And I'm pissing on your overcoat."

"Oh, Paddy," his wife bemoaned, "that drinking will drive you to your grave."

"Well," the Irishman replied as he took another sip of whiskey, "isn't that better than walking?"

Sean O'Malley was weaving his way down the street when he smacked into Father Shannon. The priest sniffed, then said sternly, "Mr. O'Malley, my nose tells me that you just came out of that devil den, the pub down the street."

O'Malley grinned. "Why, Father, would you have me spend all of my time inside?"

Eamonn O'Riley and his buddy, Paddy O'Shea, were staggering down the street when Eamonn said, "Say, let's head over to the Green Clover."

"Is that a good place?"

"Best tables I've ever been under," O'Riley swore.

A new couple moved next door, and Paddy O'Shea took it upon himself to go over and welcome them to the neighborhood. About five hours later, he made his way home and up to his bedroom. As he noisily undressed, his wife said, "So, Paddy, how are the new neighbors?"

"Nice enough folks," he replied. "But they have terrible taste. They had a quart of the worst whiskey I've ever had. I'll tell you, I nearly left a drop or two."

How can you tell an Irish drunk at the zoo? He's pounding on the bars of the lion cage shouting, "Let me out! Let me out!"

O'Malley was returning to Dublin from a pilgrimage to Lourdes. He opened his suitcase for customs. The inspector looked inside, then asked, "Sir, what's in these bottles?"

O'Malley said, "Lourdes water."

The inspector was still suspicious. He picked up a bottle, uncapped it, sniffed, then said, "Why, this is whiskey, not water."

O'Malley immediately went to his knees, looked up at Heaven, and said, "Lord, thank you for this miracle."

The Irish lodger came in blind drunk one night. The next morning, he staggered down to breakfast. The landlady looked at him, then said in a superior voice, "Mr. Shaughnessy, how do you find yourself this morning?"

"Same as yesterday," the Irishman replied. "I just threw back the sheets, and there I was."

Two Irish guys walk into a bar. Each one orders two whiskeys and immediately downs them. They motion the bartender over, order two more apiece, and those two disappear. Then the bartender is summoned for a third round. When the shot glasses are placed on the bar, one Irishman hoists a glass, turns to his friend, and says, "Cheers."

The other Irishman growls, "Hey, did you come here to bullshit or did you come here to drink?"

Two Irishmen were out drinking when they ran out of money. One said to the other, "Let's go by my place and get some money from my wife."

They staggered down the street to the man's house, went inside, and flicked on the lights. To the surprise of the homeowner's friend, the wife was on the couch, naked, making love to another man. Her husband, however, seemed oblivious. He asked, "Darling, would you have some money we can have?"

She said, "My purse is on the chair."

Her husband opened the purse, then smiled, "Ah, the cost of a pint of whiskey for you and a pint of whiskey for me."

The friend said, "But what about that guy with your wife?"

"Let him find the money for his own pint," the Irishman snapped.

What does an Irishman think of water?
That it's okay, if taken with the right spirit.

The cop was interrogating the very inebriated Irishman, who was also bleeding profusely. The cop said, "Can you describe the man who did this?"

The Irishman said, "That's what I was doing when he hit me."

What do you know about an Irishman who comes home half in the bag?
He ran out of money.

Did you hear about the new Irish organization, AAA-AA?
It's for people who want to be driven to drink.

An Irish drunk was sitting at the bar when a guy sat down next to him. The Irishman asked, "Say, do you have the time?"

"Five o'clock," the man replied.

The Irishman shook his head. "I've asked that question all day long, and every time I get a different answer."

Two Irish drunks ran out of money long before the evening was over. They were bemoaning their fate when one had an idea. He found three quarters in his pocket and used them to buy a hot dog. Then he whispered the plan into his friend Paddy's ear.

A few minutes later, they were sitting in a bar. They ordered two double whiskeys and downed them in a gulp. As the bartender came over to collect the money, the Irishman unzipped his fly and stuck the hot dog out. Paddy knelt down and began to suck it. The bartender's face turned red and he screamed, "Get out of here, you fucking fags!"

The Irishmen got outside and began to laugh hysterically. They worked the same scam in the next bar, and the next bar, and in a fourth bar. Flying high, they sat on a park bench. Paddy turned to his friend and said, "Amazing what you can get with a hot dog."

His friend said, "Hot dog, hell! I lost that after the first bar."

An Irishman was sitting outside a bar crying his eyes out. A priest walked by and said, "My son, what's wrong?"

"It's my wife," the Irishman said. "I sold her for the price of a case of Irish whiskey."

"That's horrible!" the priest exclaimed. "But God will forgive you, because it's obvious you want her back again."

"Oh, I do," the Irishman said. "I'm thirsty again."

Did you hear that Irishmen have no respect for age?
Unless it's bottled.

The Irishman staggered into the bar and yelled out, "Happy New Year!"

The bartender said, "You sot. It's February 15."

The Irishman's face fell. "My old lady's going to kill me for being out this long!"

Why don't Irishmen drink and drive?
If they hit a bump, they'd spill it.

Did you hear about the Irishman who gave up drinking?
It was the longest twenty minutes he'd ever spent.

A pink elephant, three green snakes, and a yellow rhinoceros walked into a bar. The bartender said, "You're early. Paddy's not here yet."

An Irishman was staggering through the park when he passed out on the grass. He awakened to find a grasshopper on his stomach. He looked at the insect, then said, "Hey, do you know they named a drink after you?"

To his amazement, the grasshopper said, "You're kidding? A drink named Joe?"

The Irishman woke up one morning moaning and wailing about his awful headache. His wife said, "If you can't stand the hangover, why did you get drunk in the first place?"

He retorted indignantly, "I didn't get drunk in the first place. I got drunk in the last place."

Why don't Irish drunks mind muggers?
The only way they can get home is if they're held up.

Why are Irishmen habitual drunkards?
Habitual thirst.

An Irishman was staggering down Main Street in the wee hours of the morning when he spotted the big clock on City Hall. A few minutes later, a cop driving by spotted him standing on the sidewalk dropping coins. The cop stopped and said, "Hey, what do you think you're doing dropping coins through the sewer grate?"

"Shewer!" the drunk slurred. "I thought I was weighing myself."

Did you hear about the Irishman who couldn't find his glasses?
He drank from the bottle instead.

A couple of Irishmen were fed up with paying a fortune for their numerous pints every month, so they decided to brew their own beer. They borrowed a few books from the library, pored over them, gathered the necessary ingredients, and mixed up their first batch.

The wait until it was ready was excruciating. When they opened the keg, they were so proud they decided to take a pint to the local pubkeeper, who they hoped would purchase a quantity of the brew. They handed the pint to the Irishman, who took a sip, swished it around in his mouth, and swallowed.

"Well," one of the brewers said, "what do you think?"

The pubkeeper replied, "I think your horse has diabetes."

Did you hear about the Irish woman whose doctor told her not to touch anything alcoholic?
She threw her husband out of the house.

How can you tell an Irish yuppie?
He's got whiskey in his Water Pik.

Did you hear about the six Irishmen who went
on a hunting trip?
In just three days, they killed twenty-one bottles
of whiskey.

How did the Irishman celebrate his vasectomy?
With a bottle of Dry Sac.

CHAPTER 2

GREAT IRISH ETHNIC JOKES

Paddy and Mick shared the first prize of $5 million in the Irish sweepstakes and were celebrating at the local pub.

After a while, Mick turned to Paddy and said, "Paddy, I've been thinking. What will we do with all those beggin' letters now that we've won?"

"No problem," Paddy replied, "we'll keep on sending them out."

An Aer Lingus plane was in trouble, and the pilot radioed, "Mayday! Mayday!"

"You're cleared for emergency landing," the tower radioed back. "Can you give us your height and your position?"

The pilot replied, "I'm about five feet eight, and I'm sitting in the front of the plane."

Did you hear about the Irishman and the Frenchman who jumped off the Eiffel Tower?
The Frenchman was killed and the Irishman got lost.

What happens when an Irish wife has a baby?
She has to get two bottles ready every night.

What's four miles long and has an asshole every two feet?
The St. Patrick's Day parade.

Why don't they have driver's education in Ireland anymore?
The mule died.

Why did the Irishman marry a girl born on February 29?
So he'd only have to buy her a birthday present every four years.

Why did the Irishman think he was built upside down?
Because his nose ran and his feet smelled.

How do you tell a guy is Irish?
He takes an entire bottle of Ex-Lax so he'll have something to do.

What is an average Irishman's favorite turn-on?
A hunk of corned beef and a six-pack.

How do you know a guy's Irish?
When a hooker tells him she's got a headache.

How do you tell a guy is Irish?
His hand falls asleep when he's masturbating.

Did you hear about the Irishman who finally
turned to liquor as a substitute for woman?
He got his dick caught in the mouth of a
whiskey bottle.

An Irishman went on vacation with his swinger
friend. They were sunning on the beach when,
to the Irishman's surprise, a gorgeous girl walked
by and winked at him.

"Quick, what should I do?" he asked his
friend.

"Wink back."

The Irishman winked back. The girl winked
back and smiled.

"What should I do?" the loser asked again.

"Smile back."

The Irishman smiled back. Then the girl turned
to face him, took off the top of her bikini, and
lowered her panties.

The Irishman's eyes nearly came out of his
head. "What should I do?" he demanded.

"Show her your nuts," the friend said.

So the Irishman stood up, put his thumbs in
his ears, stuck out his tongue, and went "Blah . . .
blah . . . blahhhhhh."

How can you tell Irishmen have weak bladders?
Rusty zippers and yellow socks.

Did you hear about the Irishman who was
arrested for attempted rape?
The charge was "assault with a dead weapon."

What do you call a single Irishman?
Nobody's fool.

What's an Irish fifty-piece dinner set?
Fifty toothpicks.

Why did the Irishman give hot water to his hens?
He wanted them to lay hard-boiled eggs.

How do Irishmen feel about being buried in an
English cemetery?
They'd rather die first!

Why was the Irishman's fiancée so furious when
he gave her a diamond ring?
The diamond was a sham rock.

What's Irish and comes out in the springtime?
Patty O'Furniture.

How can you tell if a guy picking his nose is Irish or Polish?
If he says grace first, he's Irish.

Two Irish mothers were talking about their sons. The first said, "My Patrick is such a saint. He works hard, doesn't smoke, and he hasn't so much as looked at a woman in over two years."

The other woman said, "Well, my Francis is a saint himself. Not only hasn't he not looked at a woman in over three years, but he hasn't touched a drop of liquor in all that time."

"My word," the first Irish mother said. "You must be so proud."

"I am," the second mother said. "And when he's paroled next month, I'm going to throw him a big party."

Why did the Irish National Symphony cancel its performances?
They lost the kazoo.

How can you tell you're in an Irish town?
Outside the pub they have pay bushes.

What do they call diarrhea in Ireland?
Brain drain.

What's the worst advice you can give an Irishman going to a job interview?
Be yourself.

How does an Irishman take a shower?
He pees in a fan.

How can you tell a psychiatrist is Irish?
Instead of a couch, he's got a Murphy bed.

What's true happiness to an Irishman?
A "No Tipping" sign in the pub.

One Irish codger was sitting in the pub when he said to a friend, "Will you look at young O'Rourke over there? The lad's such a lazy sot, he's been on that stool all day draining one pint after another."

The friend asked, "How do you know?"

"I've been sitting here watching him," the first codger replied.

A neighbor smelled smoke, so he rushed over to the O'Malleys'. To his shock, he saw their cottage in flames and O'Malley himself sitting under a tree pulling away at a bottle of Irish whiskey. The neighbor turned to him and shouted,

"For god's sakes, man, why don't you do something?"

"I am," O'Malley replied. "I've been praying for rain as hard as I can."

What's the best reason to hire an Irishman?
When he goes on vacation, you don't have to hire a replacement to do his work.

When is the only time an Irishman tells the truth?
When he admits he's lying.

How dull is Ireland?
They print the newspaper two weeks in advance.

Jack was surprised one day when he saw his friend Patrick McCree driving a brand-new car. He waved him over, then said, "Patrick, how did you get that car?"

The Irishman said, "I was drinking in the pub last night when this woman Kathleen got very friendly. At closing time, she bought us a bottle, then we got in this car and drove out into the country. I kissed her a few times, and she told me I could have anything I wanted."

"So?"

"So I took her car," the Irishman replied.

An Irishman picked up the phone, dialed the international operator, and asked how much it would cost to call New York.

"Nine dollars for three minutes," she replied.

"Begorrah!" the Irishman swore. "I can call hell and back for that amount of money."

"Yes, sir," the operator replied. "But that's a local call."

What do they call an Irishman with indoor plumbing?
Kinky.

Why did the Irish Parliament cancel St. Patrick's Day?
They dug up his body and discovered he died of sickle cell anemia.

Why are Irish men like eggs?
They're either fresh, rotten, or hard-boiled.

What's the easiest way to meet someone in an Irish bar?
Pick up their change.

What was the name of the Irish version of "Roots"?
"Weeds."

An Irishman walked into a bar with a frog on his head. The bartender said, "Now where did you get that?"

The frog replied, "I don't know. It started out as a wart on my ass."

What's the best-selling brand of tooth cleaner in Ireland?
Sandpaper.

What's the difference between an Irish wedding and an Irish funeral?
One less drunk.

One man turned to another at a bar and said, "I hear they arrested Paddy again. How does it feel to have a thief in the family?"

The second man was offended. "Paddy's not a thief. He's just got a talent for finding things. It's not his fault that he finds them before they're lost."

A woman was driving down a narrow back road in Ireland when her way was blocked by a donkey cart. She got out of the car and walked up to an Irish farm lad who was trying to get the beast to move. She sized up the situation and said, "Mind if I try to get the donkey to move?"

"It's all right with me."

The woman reached between the donkey's legs and squeezed. Immediately the animal took off in a sprint.

"What did you do?" the Irish lad said.

"I pinched his balls," the woman said.

The Irish lad immediately dropped his pants and said, "Well, you'd better pinch mine—I've got to catch him."

The cross-Atlantic flight was very long, and the very proper English lady was increasingly disconcerted by the Irishman next to her, whose conversation became increasingly colorful the more he drank. Finally she said to him, "I would appreciate your remaining totally silent for the rest of the flight. We do not agree on one single thing."

"I don't know about that," the Irishman offered. "I'll give you an example. If you walked into a bedroom and found a naked man in one bed and a naked woman in the other bed, who would you sleep with?"

Shocked, she replied, "Why, the woman, of course."

He said, "See, we agree. So would I."

What's wrong with meeting people in Irish bars?

In the bars, the men are all stiff and the women

are all tight, but when you get them home, neither is.

Mrs. Muldoon came in from the farm to sell butter to O'Shaughnessy. He put the crock on the scale, then said, "Why, Mrs. Muldoon, I can't believe you tried to cheat me. You said this butter weighed ten pounds, but on my scale it's only seven."

"You're the rascal," the farm lady retorted. "I weighed the butter against the ten pounds of sugar you sold me last week."

Two Irishmen were stranded for days on an iceberg. They were near death when one jumped up and said, "Paddy, Paddy, we're saved! Here comes a ship."

"Wonderful. What's its name?"

"It's hard to read. But I think it's the *Titanic*."

An Irishman was called into court for destroying a bar in a brawl. He appeared before the judge, who asked, "So what do you have to say for yourself?"

The Irishman said, "Your Honor, I'm not guilty. My reputation is spotless."

The judge said, "Do you have any witnesses that can vouch for your character?"

The Irishman pointed to a man in the corner. "The sheriff over there."

The sheriff stood up and said, "Your Honor, the man's a liar. I've never seen him before in my life."

The Irishman turned to the judge and said, "See, I've lived in this town for fifteen years and the sheriff doesn't know me. Isn't that character enough?"

Why did they cancel the Irish National Steeplechase? None of the horses could get up the cathedral roof.

Late one night, Paddy O'Rourke suddenly fell off his bar stool, dead from a massive heart attack. All his buddies spent two hours arguing about how to tell his wife. Finally, Patrick McCarthy drew the short straw, and knocked at the man's door.

It took awhile, but finally Mrs. O'Rourke opened the door and said, "What do you want?"

McCarthy said, "I wanted to tell you that your husband got drunk and lost his whole paycheck in a card game."

Her eyes blazed. "That sot. He should drop dead."

McCarthy said, "Funny you should mention that. He did."

How was the bagpipe invented?
The Irish sold them to the Scots for a joke, and the Scots haven't gotten the joke yet.

A guy walked into a bar, ordered a beer, then said, "Hey, listen, everybody. I got some great Irish jokes."

The bartender came over and said sternly, "Listen, Mac. I'm Irish. Those two guys to your left are Irish. And those two huge truck drivers at the table over there are Irish. You get what I mean?"

"Sure," the guy said. "I'll tell them very slowly."

A Jew, a Hindu, and an Irishman were traveling in the countryside when a storm hit. They sought refuge for the night at a local farmhouse. The farmer said, "I'll be glad to put you up, but I only have two extra beds. One of you will have to sleep in the barn with the cow and the pig."

The men drew straws, and the Jew headed for the barn. A few minutes later, he knocked on the door and said, "I'm sorry. But my religion prohibits me from sleeping with a pig."

So the Hindu headed for the barn. But a few minutes later, he knocked on the door and said, "In my religion, cows are sacred. I can't sleep with one."

The Irishman grumbled, but he headed for the

barn. A few minutes later, the cow and pig knocked on the door.

Did you hear about the World Cup soccer match between Scotland and Ireland?
The Scottish team walked off the field. Twenty minutes later, the Irish team scored.

A Jew, a Frenchman, and an Irishman survived a shipwreck, but were stranded on a deserted island. One day they were walking on the beach when they found a bottle. They picked it up, and a genie appeared. The genie said, "I will grant each of you a wish."
The Jew said, "I wish I were back in my diamond business in New York City." There was a puff of smoke, and he disappeared.
The Frenchman said, "I wish I was in my mistress's arms in Paris." There was a puff of smoke, and he disappeared.
The Irishman licked his lips and said, "I miss those guys. I wish they were here joining me in a pint."

What do you call three Irishman sitting on the lawn?
Fertilizer.

What do you call an Irish homosexual?
Gay-lick.

Two Irishmen sat in silence side by side at the bar, downing one drink after another. Finally one turned to the other and said, "Paddy, I've finally got it figured out. It's a dog-eat-dog world."

Paddy reflected for about an hour. Then he said, "Maybe you've got something there. Then again, maybe it's the other way around."

An Irishman had been stranded on a deserted island for ten years. To his great surprise, he was standing on the beach one day and saw a human being clinging to a piece of driftwood. He dashed into the surf, and pulled to the shore a beautiful young woman dressed in tattered clothing and clutching a waterproof bag.

It took awhile for the woman to regain consciousness. Then the man started to tell her the story of how he managed to survive on that island. She was stunned. "I can't believe you've been here ten years. Tell me, did you smoke cigarettes before you were stranded?"

"Yes."

She reached into her waterproof bag, pulled out a pack of cigarettes and some matches, then handed him one. He puffed away with great glee.

As he smoked, she asked, "Were you a drinking man before you were stranded?"

He said, "I loved my whiskey."

She reached into her waterproof bag, pulled out a bottle of the finest, and gave it to him. He took a long pull.

She took a look at his lean, tan body, and a thought occurred to her. She said seductively, "I guess if you're here alone you haven't had the chance to play around in ten years."

The Irishman grew very excited. "You mean," he shouted, "you've got a set of golf clubs in there?"

A traveling salesman's car broke down in a rural area of Ireland, and he walked to the nearest farm to get help. As he waited for the farmer to finish his chores, he was astounded to see a pig with one wooden leg hobbling across the barnyard. When he expressed his astonishment to the farmer, the Irishman said, "Aye, that's one pig in a million, a genuine hero. One night I'd had a few snorts too many and I fell asleep in the barn. The barn caught on fire, but I was dead to the world. That pig shooed out the other animals, then dragged me out into the barnyard."

"Amazing," the salesman said.

"That's not all," the farmer said. "The flames jumped to the house. So that pig went in and dragged out my wife and two daughters."

"That's incredible," the salesman said. "But how did the pig get that wooden leg?"

The Irishman said, "Pig like that, you just don't eat all at once."

An Irishman was visiting his American cousin, and they decided to go on a camping trip in Maine. The second night out, they were asleep in their tent when the cousin screamed. The Irishman asked him what happened.

"A rattlesnake bit me on the cock. You've got to help me."

Since St. Patrick had driven all snakes out of Ireland long ago, the Irishman had no idea what to do. So he ran as fast as he could three miles back to the highway, flagged down a car, then got dropped off at a phone booth. He dialed a doctor, then explained the situation.

The doctor said, "Listen carefully. You take your pocket knife, carefully cut an X into the skin where the snake bit, and suck out all the venom. But it has to be done quickly or the bite is fatal."

The Irishman thanked him, hitched a ride back, ran three miles through the woods, and found his cousin writhing in pain. The cousin said through clenched teeth, "What did the doctor say?"

"He said you're going to die."

An American was in Ireland on business, and one day he decided to take a drive through the countryside. He was admiring the scenery on a back road when his way was blocked by a fallen tree. He stopped the car. To his horror, an Irishman carrying an automatic rifle stepped in front of him and ordered him out of the car.

The terrified businessman said, "If you want money, my wallet's in the glove compartment."

The Irishman ignored him. He commanded, "Drop your pants and beat off."

The American was about to protest, but the Irishman pointed the weapon at his crotch. So he did what he was told. When he was finished, he asked, "Now what?"

The Irishman said, "Do it again."

The American had a tougher time, but he managed to comply. He was a bit flushed when the Irishman said, "Do it a third time." The businessman started to protest, but the Irishman stuck the rifle in his ear.

The third time took nearly half an hour. The businessman was so spent he didn't see the Irishman lower the rifle. He was about to ask what was going on when the Irishman said, "Okay. Now I want you to give my daughter a ride to Dublin."

How lazy was the Irishman?
He took his bride to San Francisco and waited for an earthquake.

What did the bull say to the nearsighted Irish milkmaid?
"Mooooooooo!!!!"

Why do so many Irish men marry Australian girls?
They're nicer down under.

Two Irishmen arrived in New York, and walked around gazing at the sights of the city. They eventually landed in a bar and were sipping their beers when the bartender said, "We've got free lunch today, fellows. Hot dogs are on that table over there."

One Irishman said, "Thanks." Then he turned to his friend and said, "These Yanks eat dogs?"

The other guy shrugged and said, "Let's try it." So they got up, went over to the table, and returned with the lunch they were served. They sat in silence for a second, then one turned to the other and said, "What part of the dog did you get?"

An American, an Englishman, and an Irishman were driving in the country when their car broke down. They walked to a farmhouse and asked to spend the night. The farmer had three young daughters, so he at first refused. But finally he said, "You can sleep in the loft in the barn. But I'll be sleeping downstairs with my shotgun, and if you take so much as one step down the ladder, I'll shoot you."

The three men agreed and went to sleep. But in the middle of the night, the American woke up with a full bladder. He quietly made his way down the ladder. Suddenly he heard a shotgun cocking, then the farmer shouted, "Who's there?" Thinking quickly, the American went, "Meow." The farmer thought it was a cat and went back to sleep.

An hour later, the Englishman had the same need. He crept down the ladder. Once again the shotgun cocked and the farmer shouted, "Who's there?" The Englishman went, "Meow." The farmer thought it was a cat again, and went back to sleep.

An hour later, the Irishman had to relieve himself. He crept down the ladder. The shotgun cocked, and the farmer shouted, "Who's there?" The Irishman replied, "It's me, the cat."

An Irishman was walking through the woods when he stumbled over a sleeping leprechaun. The leprechaun was grumpy at being awakened, but he went along with his duty. He told the Irishman, "You can have your one wish for seeing me."

The Irishman said, "I'd like my dick to touch the ground."

The leprechaun grinned, then cut off his legs.

A grave digger had just finished his job and pulled the ladder out of the hole when he slipped and tumbled back in. He had no way to get out, so he periodically shouted. But no one heard him, and night fell.

In the wee hours of the morning, Paddy O'Shea stumbled out of the tavern and decided to take a shortcut through the cemetery. He was halfway through when he heard the grave digger shout, "Please help me. I'm so cold."

Paddy staggered over to the edge of the grave and said, "No wonder. You don't have any dirt over you."

A guy was walking down the street when he saw an Irishman frantically searching every pub. He went up to him and asked, "Sean, what's the problem?"

"I lost my wallet."

"Ah. So you're looking for your wallet?"

"No," the Irishman said. "My brother found my wallet."

The guy was puzzled. "Why, that's terrific. But what are you looking for now?"

"My brother," the Irishman replied.

How can you tell an Irishman in a fancy French restaurant?
He's the one trying to decide what wine goes best with whiskey.

CHAPTER 3

GREAT JOKES ABOUT THE IRISH AND RELIGION

An Irishman moved to London and got a job as a messenger. The first day he was sent to the Bank of England. The doorman directed him to a clerk, who asked, "Sir, do you want a redemption or a conversion?"

The Irishman was startled. "I must be in the wrong place. I wanted the Bank of England, not the Church of England."

The Irish cop was called to the twentieth floor of the building, where a man was standing on a ledge outside a window. The cop leaned out and said, "Don't jump, man. Think of your wife and children."

The man replied, "I don't have a wife or children."

"Then think of your parents," the cop said.

"My parents are dead," the man said.

The cop thought for a moment, then said, "Well, think of what good St. Patrick would think of this."

"Who's St. Patrick?" the man asked.

"Go on and jump, you bastard," the cop said.

Why do Irish nuns get tired of their lives?
It's the same thing, wick in and wick out.

Two Irish nuns were walking into town when a man leaped out of the bushes. He pulled one to the ground and raped her. When it was over, one nun turned to the other and asked, "What are we going to do? How can I explain to Mother Superior I was raped twice in one night?"

"Twice?" the puzzled sister asked.

"Well, we are coming back this way, aren't we?"

What do Irish nuns and 7-Up have in common?
"Never had it, never will."

What happened to the nun who got tired of using candles?
She called in an electrician.

The evil leprechaun thought he'd have some fun one day, so he popped over to the golf course. He spotted one poor player mired in a sand trap. As he moved closer, he learned from the conversation among the foursome that the player in the trap was trailing badly in a big-money match. So the leprechaun appeared to the golfer and said, "My son, I have magic powers.

I'll turn you into a world-champion golfer. But there's one catch."

"What's that?" the golfer asked.

"You will never be able to see a woman naked, have sex, or marry for the rest of your life."

The golfer said, "I'll do it if you guarantee I'll win this match."

The leprechaun agreed. The golfer swung his club, and to his astonishment, the ball flew from the trap and into the hole.

An hour later, the leprechaun came into the locker room to see the golfer celebrating with a big pint of stout. Eager to see if he regretted the deal yet, the leprechaun went up to him and said, "I need your name to complete my record of this deal."

"Okay," the golfer said, "I'm Father Patrick Murphy."

The priest came out of the confessional one day to see a small boy sitting right outside. The priest said sternly, "Young man, how dare you listen to all the confessions?"

The boy said, "Father, I didn't listen to all the confessions. I swear."

"I hope not," the priest said.

"Honest," the boy added. "I came just as that girl was confessing that she screwed the bus driver."

Sister Kathleen and Sister Francis Mary were walking down a road near the convent one night when two men jumped into the road, grabbed them, pulled them into the bushes, and began raping them. Despite her panic Sister Kathleen managed to call out, "Lord, forgive them, for they know not what they do!"

"Shut up," Sister Francis Mary called. "This one certainly does!"

A guy in a hurry to get to a golf date ran a red light. His car smacked into another car, and both cars rolled over completely. The guilty driver pried himself out of his car, then turned. To his amazement, the driver who staggered from the other vehicle was Father McCarthy. He rushed over to the dazed priest and said, "Father, I'm very sorry."

"By the saints of Ireland," the priest said, "you nearly killed me. You were tearing around like the devil himself."

"I know, Father," the guy said. Then something occurred to him. He turned to the priest and said, "Father, you're pale as a ghost. I've got a bottle of medicinal Jamieson in my car. A dose would do you good."

The priest's face brightened. "Perhaps it would."

The guy fetched the bottle and handed it to Father McCarthy, who took a healthy chug. Then he said, "I can't believe you drove like that. I nearly met my maker."

The guy said, "Father, I'm sorry. Please have some more of my bottle there to ease my pain."

"If you insist." The priest took another healthy swig, then a third. A few minutes later, the bottle was nearly empty. Then the priest turned to the guy and said, "My son, isn't it time you joined me for a nip?"

"No thank you, Father," the man said. "I'll just sit here next to you and wait for the police."

A young Irish priest was assigned right out of the seminary to a parish near Times Square in Manhattan. On his way from the Port Authority Bus Terminal to the rectory, he passed a legion of scantily clad hookers, who kept saying, "Hey, Father. How about twenty dollars for a blow job?"

The startled young man finally arrived at his new home. A little way later, the Mother Superior came to greet him. After a few minutes the priest said, "I hope you don't mind if I ask you a question. What's a blow job?"

The nun said, "It's twenty dollars, at least in this neighborhood."

The priest heard that the new Irish family in the parish was blessed with a new arrival. He stopped by the house and said to the father, "I'd like to schedule the christening as soon as possible."

"No way!" Paddy exclaimed. "We had three other babies die doing that."

The puzzled priest asked, "How could a baby die from being bathed in holy water?"

"It weren't the water," the Irishman replied. "It was hitting them over the head with the bottle."

What's black and white and black and white and black and white and black and white and black and white and black and white and black and white and black and white? A nun falling down the stairs.

Two slightly inebriated Irishmen arrived at the door of the convent late one Friday evening. They banged loudly until a nun opened the door. They told the nun that they had to speak with Mother Superior about a very urgent matter.

The Reverend Mother was summoned. One Irishman removed his hat respectfully, then asked, "Excuse me, your holiness, but do you have any midget nuns in the convent?"

"Why, no, we do not," she replied. The two men whispered for a moment, then the first asked, "Sister, do you know of any midget nuns in any of the neighboring parishes?"

Again the reply was negative. The two men whispered once more, then the man asked, "If I could ask one more question, Reverend Mother

—do you know of any midget nuns in the whole of Ireland?"

"No, I do not."

The first man turned, slapped the other across the face, then shouted, "I told you, dummy, you fucked a penguin!"

What's the newest rage among Irish nuns?
A vibrating crucifix.

What did the Bishop do when young Father O'Rourke confessed he was so horny that he was constantly aroused?
Got down on his knees, offered a prayer to God, then licked the problem.

Why do Irish priests have no problems believing in the Holy Spirit?
Most of them are fairies.

A girl was sexually attacked in an alley in New York City. The would-be rapist tore off her clothes, but she managed to evade his clutches and run away. She dashed into the street to flag down a car. A taxi slowed, but banged into her anyway. She fell to the sidewalk, unconscious.

The taxi driver jumped out of his vehicle. Embarrassed for her because she was naked, he took off his hat and placed it over her crotch. The he started CPR to revive her as a crowd gathered.

A moment later, Father McCarthy, who'd been in a nearby pub, saw the commotion. A member of the crowd said, "Father, there's a girl hurt." The priest made his way through the crowd, then saw the badly injured girl. The taxi driver saw him and asked, "Father, what should we do?"

Father McCarthy pointed to the hat and said, "My son, the first thing is we have to get that poor chap out of there."

The obviously pregnant young nun was called into the Mother Superior. "Can you explain this, Sister Francis Mary?" the Mother Superior demanded.

"I went to Father McCarthy to confess my impure thoughts. He said the only way to purge those thoughts was to let him touch me. I didn't want to, but he showed me where it was written in the Scriptures."

The Mother Superior said, "I don't know anywhere in the Holy Bible where this type of conduct is condoned."

"Right here," the nun said, opening the Bible. "It reads, 'Thy rod and thy staff shall comfort me . . .' "

When did the young Irish girl leave the convent?
When she discovered "nun" really meant "none."

Why are so many Irish priests drunks?
They're drawn to the pure in spirit.

A young female gymnast went to confession one morning right after practice. She was so happy at receiving absolution that she came out of the confessional, took a running start down the aisle, then did a series of back flips.

Mrs. O'Malley, who was waiting in the confession line, turned to her friend and said, "Glory be, would you look what Father Shannon is giving for penance today. And of all days for me not to be wearing my panties!"

The new bride wanted to make sure that she was doing everything properly. So she went to confession one Saturday and asked Father McCarthy, "Father, is it all right to have intercourse before communion?"

"Certainly, my dear," the priest replied. "As long as we don't make too much noise."

The very naive young nun was assigned to a rural Irish parish. On the first Saturday, Father Shannon asked her if she wanted to go swimming.

She'd never been before, but the priest promised he'd give her lessons.

They changed into bathing suits, then the priest offered her a hand as they entered the water. They splashed around for a few minutes until the nun turned to the priest and asked, "Father, will I really drown if you take your fingers out of my hole?"

Paddy hadn't been to church in many years, but one Sunday his wife's nagging finally got to him. She dragged him into mass on a hot August day, then constantly poked him with instructions such as, "Sit. Kneel. Stand up. Sit down."

Finally he was getting fed up. He took out his handkerchief, wiped his brow, then dropped it in his lap. Noticing the handkerchief's placement, his wife asked, "Is your fly open?"

"No," he responded wearily. "Should it be?"

Father McCarthy was in New York for a Catholic school conference. On his first evening, he went down to the lobby and wandered around. Then he spotted Colleen, a very shapely cigarette girl. He went over to her and asked, "Are you Catholic, my dear?"

"Yes, Father," she replied.

"Well, then," the priest said, "I have to ask you to go up to my room with me right now."

"Father!" she protested, shocked.

"Don't be upset," he said. "It's in the Bible."

Obediently she followed him up to his room. When they got there, he said, "My child, take off all your clothes."

She blushed. "I . . . I can't."

The priest said, "My dear, it's in the Bible."

So she obeyed. Then Father McCarthy took off his clothes and said, "Now, let's go to bed." When he saw the look in her eyes, he added, "It's in the Bible."

So she hopped in the sack and they made love. Afterward, Colleen said, "Father, that was terrific. But I'm going to have to go to confession unless you show me exactly what it says in the Bible."

The priest reached in the drawer of the table by the bed, pulled out the Bible, opened to a page, and said, "See here, my dear. It says, 'The cigarette girl screws.' "

The day started out sunny and calm, and all of the guests on the sailboat were laughing and joking. Suddenly clouds loomed on the horizon, and before they could make it back to shore, a storm struck. The passengers clung for dear life as the wind howled and the waves threatened to overturn the craft.

In desperation one woman called out to an

Irishman who was clinging to a rope near her, "Only God can help us. Do something religious."

So he started a bingo game.

The old Irishman had never turned down a drink, and he was three sheets to the wind one night when he met Sister Mary Francis walking down the street. The nun took one look and said, "The Lord save me, you're supposed to be dead."

O'Malley stopped, looked at her, and said, "I'm as alive as you. What fool told you I was dead?"

The sister glared at him. "Why, Father Murphy told me. And since his reputation is far better than yours, you must be dead."

The priest was giving a sermon in the park when he was heckled by an atheist who shouted, "How do you know that Joseph was the father of your Jesus?"

The priest replied, "Well, when I get to Heaven, I'll ask him."

The unbeliever retorted, "And what if he isn't in Heaven."

The priest said, "Then you ask him."

The priest was talking to some parishioners one day when Paddy wandered by, drunk. He listened for a moment, then interrupted to say, "Father, you're always talking about miracles. What the hell is a miracle?"

The priest said, "Bend over and I'll show you."

Paddy bent over, and the priest gave him a tremendous kick between his legs. Paddy howled in pain, dropped to the ground, and writhed around. When he had regained some composure, the priest asked, "Paddy, did you feel that?"

"Of course I did," the Irishman stammered.

"If you hadn't," the priest said, "that would have been a miracle."

Two Irish ladies were sitting on the stoop, watching men go in and out of the brothel across the street. After an hour, they saw a rabbi walk down the street, go up the steps, and enter the house of ill repute. One lady turned and said, "Those Jews are all perverts."

Another twenty minutes passed. Then a Protestant minister walked down the street and entered the whorehouse. The lady said, "The state of the clergy today is disgraceful."

Yet another twenty minutes passed. Then a priest appeared, walked past them, and entered the brothel. The lady turned to her friend and said, "Glory be, one of the girls must be very, very sick."

Paddy O'Toole was staggering down the street. He barely managed to keep his feet when he reached the cathedral. He took a look, then stumbled up the steps, through the front door, and down the aisle. He gazed around drunkenly, then opened the door to one of the confessional booths and entered.

The priest was hearing the confession of a woman in the booth on the other side. Noticing the commotion, he slid open the window on the drunk's side and said, "I'll be with you in a moment, my son."

The drunk said, "I don't need help. I just want to know if you have any paper in that stall."

A little Irish boy was throwing a huge tantrum in church as his mother waited for confession. No one could calm him until the priest came out of the confessional, went over, and whispered in the boy's ear. Immediately the tot was quiet as a mouse.

A few minutes later, the boy's amazed mother entered the confessional. She said to the priest, "Father, before we start, I have to know what you said to calm Ryan like that."

The priest said, "I pointed to the crucifix over the altar. And I told him the guy hanging on it was the last person who screamed in this church."

The nun who taught third grade in the Belfast Catholic school was asking the children what they wanted to be when they grew up. One little boy said, "I want to be a carpenter."

"Good," the sister replied. "And you, Maureen?"

"I want to be a nurse."

"Good. And you, Bridget?"

"I want to be a prostitute."

"That's horrible," the nun shrieked. "You'll be damned to eternal perdition. I should tear your eyes out right here!"

"Just because I want to be a prostitute?"

The nun gave a sigh of relief, "Oh, I'm sorry, my dear girl," she said. "I thought you said 'Protestant.' "

What's black and white and has a hole in the middle?
An Irish nun.

When an Irishman makes the sign of the cross, what's he most thankful for?
That they crucified Christ instead of castrating him.

How do you know you're in an Irish bar?
You call a telephone number on the men's room wall and get Dial-a-Prayer.

CHAPTER 4

GREAT JOKES ABOUT DUMB IRISHMEN

How do you make an Irishman laugh on
Monday?
Tell him a joke on Friday.

What do you call an Irishman with half a brain?
"Mr. Prime Minister."

What's the difference between an Irish library and
an Irish telephone booth?
An Irish telephone booth has a book in it.

Did you hear about the really dumb Irishman?
He parked his car in front of the loan company.

Why did the Irishman sue the baker?
For forging his signature on a hot cross bun.

Did you hear about the Irish guy who was given
three weeks to live?
He took the first two weeks in July and the last
week in December.

What's it called when you play a game of wits with an Irishman?
Solitaire.

What is an Irish jigsaw puzzle?
One piece.

Why was the little Irish kid so upset when the label fell off his yellow crayon?
He wanted to know what color it was.

Did you hear about the Irish kid whose teacher ordered the class to write a two-hundred-word essay on what they did during summer vacation?
He wrote "Not much" one hundred times.

An American, an Englishman, and an Irishman were hiking in the mountains of Asia when they heard the legend of a magic cliff that had strange powers. They fought through ice and snow and wind until they found the cliff. Sure enough, when they stood on the edge and looked down thousands of feet, a genie appeared and said, "To obtain your heart's desire, just shout your wish and jump off the cliff."

The three were hesitant, but the American said, "Well, as long as we've come this far, I'll try it." He walked to the edge, yelled, "Billionaire," and jumped. Out of the clouds swooped a private jet, snatched him out of the air, and flew him away.

The Englishman stepped forward, thought for a moment, then yelled, "Harem." Suddenly he landed gently on a magic carpet filled with a dozen gorgeous women that miraculously appeared.

As the Irishman stepped forward, he tripped over a rock, tumbled off the cliff, and yelled, "Oh, shit!"

How dumb is an Irishman?
He thinks his wife has been at church when she comes home with a Gideon Bible.

An Irish bricklayer came hobbling into the doctor one morning. He told him, "I think I broke my foot."

The doctor asked, "What happened?"

The Irishman said, "Well, it started twenty-one years ago."

"Twenty-one years?" the startled doctor exclaimed.

"Yes, I'd just started as an apprentice to old Sean O'Toole, and I was sleeping in the loft of his barn. The first night, O'Toole's youngest daughter climbed up into the loft and asked if there was anything she could do for me. I said I was comfortable, and she went away."

"So?"

"The next night, she climbed up to the loft again, this time wearing her nightgown. She asked if she could do anything for me, and I said I was fine."

The doctor said, "I don't understand what this has to do with your foot."

"Well, the third night, she came up to the loft stark naked and asked if there was anything she could do for me. I said I was fine, and she left."

"I don't understand."

The Irishman explained, "This afternoon I finally realized what she was up to. I got so mad I threw a brick against the wall, and it bounced off and broke my foot."

The Irishman went to the dentist, who examined him thoroughly. Then the dentist said, "Paddy, you've got a tooth that needs pulling. But don't worry about the pain. I'll use a local anesthetic."

"Money is no object," the Irishman said. "Go ahead and use the imported stuff."

On Irish TV, what announcement do they make every night?
"It's ten o'clock. Do you know what time it is?"

What did the Irishman do when he heard that ninety percent of all serious accidents happen around home?
He moved.

Why did the Irish girl go to town?
She wanted to trade her menstrual cycle for a Honda.

Why did the Irishman climb a tree?
He wanted to be a branch manager.

The Irishman's girlfriend always wanted to fly, so for her birthday he chartered a small plane for a ride over New York City. The two strapped themselves in behind the pilot and the plane took off. As they cruised over the nation's largest city, Paddy tried to show off. He pointed to a building and said, "Hey, that's the Empire State Building."

The pilot, hearing him, leaned back and said, "Wrong, pal. That's the Chrysler Building."

The mick grimaced. A moment later he pointed and said to his girl, "Hey, that's Shea Stadium."

The pilot once again leaned back and said, "Wrong, pal. That's Yankee Stadium."

Paddy's face turned red. But before he had a chance to do anything, the engine on the plane started to sputter, then conked out. Hurriedly the pilot strapped a parachute on, then handed parachutes to the Irishman and his girlfriend. "Put these on," he said. "Then jump clear of the plane, count to ten, and pull this ripcord." Then the pilot jumped.

Paddy and his girlfriend jumped side by side.

As they cleared the plane, the girl noticed he was laughing hysterically. She shouted, "What's so funny?"

Paddy replied, "That pilot thinks he knows everything. But he didn't know I can't count to ten."

A wealthy couple hired an Irish caretaker to do some work around their estate while they toured Europe. A month later, they arrived home during a violent rainstorm. To their great horror, they walked into their living room to find the Irishman sitting in the middle of the floor while water poured from the ceiling.

"You idiot!" the man shouted. "I told you about that roof. Get up there right now and stop that leak."

"Can't," the Irishman replied. "It's raining too hard."

"Well, why didn't you fix it when it wasn't raining outside?"

"Because it wasn't leaking then."

Why did the Irish farmer cut the legs off his cow? He wanted ground beef.

The Irishman walked into the newspaper and said, "I'd like to put a funeral notice about my father in your paper."

"Certainly," the girl said. "That will be five dollars per inch."

"Oh, no," the Irishman moaned. "He was all of six feet tall."

An Irish handyman was installing new wall-to-wall carpeting in the family room of a home. He'd had a little too much to drink the night before, so he was in a bit of a daze as he worked. Finally he finished and stepped back to inspect the job. To his dismay, he noticed a lump right in the middle of the floor.

The thought of tearing up all the carpet churned his stomach. He patted his pockets for a moment, looking for a smoke. Then he realized his pack of cigarettes was missing. He checked his gear and his coat, but the cigarettes weren't there.

Then he had an idea. He got a hammer, walked into the room, and began smashing the lump. It took awhile, but finally the lump was so flattened that it was barely noticeable. Satisfied, he carried his tools out to his truck.

His pack of cigarettes was on the front seat. As he walked back into the house, he heard a little boy say, "Mommy, have you seen the kitten?"

Two Irishmen were out in a boat fishing. They discovered a spot where the fish were really biting, and they hauled in fish after fish until they were exhausted. When it was time to go home, one Irishman said to the other, "We should mark this spot so we can find it tomorrow."

"Good idea," his friend replied. "Let's make an *X* on the bottom of the boat."

His friend grimaced. "You moron. That won't work."

"Why not?"

"What if we don't get the same boat?"

A man was driving down an Irish road when he saw a young farm boy supporting the hind legs of a pig on his shoulders, so the pig could eat apples off a tree. The man stopped, watched in amazement, then got out of his car, and walked over. He said, "You know, son, you'd save a lot of time if you shook the tree, let the apples fall to the ground, then let the pig eat them."

The Irish lad shrugged. "What's time to a pig?"

A man ran up to an Irish cop and said, "Officer, someone just stole my car!"

"I know," the cop replied. "But don't you go and worry. I got the license number."

Why do Irishmen all think they're wits?
They're half right.

What's an experienced Irish secretary?
A girl who can consistently type twenty mistakes
a minute.

How do you confuse an Irishman?
Put two shovels on the ground and tell him to
take his pick.

An Irishman was standing on the curb watching
a funeral procession when a passerby asked,
"Do you know whose funeral this is?"
The Irishman replied, "I can't say for sure. But
my guess is that guy in the coffin."

What's the difference between an Irishman and
a roast beef sandwich?
A roast beef sandwich is only an inch thick.

Two Irishmen were riding in a cart pulled by a
horse when they came to a tunnel so low the
horse couldn't pass. One Irishman got out, took
a hammer, and began pounding away at the
rock arch of the tunnel.
The other Irishman said, "Paddy, wouldn't it
be easier to dig away at the mud than chip that
rock?"
"Fool," the first Irishman exclaimed. "It's not
his feet that are the problem, it's his head."

One Irishman met another coming out of the soccer stadium and asked, "What was the score?"

"It was zero, zero."

"And what was the score at halftime?"

"Couldn't tell you," the Irishman replied. "I only saw the second half."

What did the Irishman do when his boat sprung a leak at one end?
Drilled a hole at the other end to let the water out.

The Irishman was in church when the priest announced, "It is the Lord's will that you tithe, that you give a tenth of your income to do His work."

The Irishman turned to his buddy and said, "Will you listen to that? Next thing you know, he'll be asking for a twentieth."

The Irishman's store was burglarized one night. The next morning, the police came to take a statement. The Irishman said, "Well, at least it wasn't as bad as it could have been."

"How's that?"

"Yesterday everything was on sale."

An Irishman who'd had more than a couple of drinks opened the door to his bedroom to find his wife sleeping with another man. He rushed to the closet, pulled out a shotgun, cocked it, and held it to his temple.

"Don't laugh," he shouted when the man started to chuckle. "You're next."

A realtor was showing off a new million-dollar house to some prospective buyers. Every time he'd escort them into another room, he'd walk over to the window, open it, and shout, "Green side up!" Finally the buyers asked him what he was doing.

"Oh," he replied, "I've got some Irish guys laying sod for the lawn."

An Irishman was working on the saw at a lumber mill when he suddenly called out, "Boss, boss! I cut a finger off."

The boss ran over to see the Irishman's hand gushing blood. "My god, man, how did that happen?"

The Irishman said, "I was putting my hand down like this and—damn, it got another one!"

Did you hear about the Irishman who locked his keys in his car?
Took him three hours to get his family out.

An Irishman was out in the woods hunting when he came across a beautiful woman sunbathing in the nude. She waved him over, winked, then said, "Hey, sport, I'm game."

So he shot her.

Three convicts, an American, an Englishman, and an Irishman, escaped from a maximum-security prison. They dashed through the woods toward freedom, but the barking of the prison dogs steadily moved closer. Finally one convict said to the others, "Quick, we've got to hide in these trees." So each scampered up a tree.

The dogs and the guards holding them approached the base of the tree in which the American was hiding. Thinking quickly, the Yank opened his mouth and went, "Whoo. Whoo." One guard said, "It's just an owl. Let's move on."

The dogs led the guards to the tree in which the Englishman was hiding. The Englishman went, "Caw, caw, caw." A guard said, "It's just a crow. Let's move on."

The dogs led the guards to the tree in which the Irishman was hiding. The Irishman thought for a moment, then went, "Mooo. Mooo."

Did you hear about the four Irishmen who tried to build a houseboat?

They drowned digging the foundation.

How did the dumb Irishman try to get stoned?
By drinking wet cement.

Did you hear about the Irish subway worker who took a piss on the third rail?
Instantly he became a conductor.

Why did the Irishman stick his prick in his whiskey?
His wife told him to get sterilized.

Did you hear about the Irishman who fell in love with his cow?
It was udder madness.

CHAPTER 5

GREAT JOKES ABOUT THE IRISH REPUBLICAN ARMY

What do most people in Irish hospitals have in common?
They're all IRA explosives experts.

How does the son in an IRA family know when his father passes away?
The lights dim.

A man walked out of a house in Belfast, Northern Ireland, one night. He turned a corner, then found himself confronted by an armed masked man pointing an automatic weapon. "Halt," the man said. "Are you Protestant or Catholic?"

Immediately the man breathed a sigh of relief. "Neither," he replied. "I'm Jewish."

The gunman pressed the trigger, riddling him with bullets. Then he removed himself and said, "I must be the luckiest Arab in Ireland tonight."

What's the worst mistake you can make when you plan a party?
Hiring an IRA member to blow up the balloons.

Two IRA members were driving through the streets of Belfast when one turned to the other nervously and asked, "Sean, what if the bomb in the backseat blows up before we get there?"

Sean smiled. "Don't worry. I've got a spare in the trunk."

The Protestant politician was up on the dais blasting the IRA. He shouted, "Show me a member of the Irish Republican Army, and I'll show you a coward."

Suddenly a big, burly man with a huge bulge under his coat stepped forward and said, "I'm an IRA man."

"Take a look at a coward," the Protestant said as he sprinted away.

Why is teenage sex so exciting in Belfast?
You don't know if the car's going to explode before you do.

How many IRA members does it take to change a light bulb?
None. They just stand around and threaten it.

How do you know your cabdriver is a member of the IRA?
You find yourself tied up in traffic.

What's so strange about drinking in Belfast?
You stay sober, but the bar gets blasted.

What's made of metal, glass, and rubber, and
comes in five thousand parts?
A used car in Belfast.

Did you hear that General Motors is making a
new car called the Belfast?
It comes with factory-installed pipe bombs.

Who are the nattiest men in the world?
Members of the IRA—they're always dressed to
kill.

What happened when the IRA guy tried to blow
up a bus?
He burned his lips on the exhaust pipe.

   The IRA member woke up slowly. He groaned,
then opened his eyes. To his amazement, he was
in a hospital bed. He started to stir when a voice
said, "Don't try to move."
   The IRA man saw a doctor standing over him.
He said, "Doc, what's wrong with me?"
   The doctor said, "Well, I've got some good
news and some bad news."

"Gimme the bad news."

"The bad news is that the bomb you were carrying blew up early and you lost both of your feet."

"Oh, God!" the IRA man exclaimed. "That's terrible. What could possibly be the good news?"

"The guy in the next room wants to buy your shoes."

St. Peter was logging in the new arrivals at the Pearly Gates when a strapping young Irishman stepped in front of him. "What do you think you're doing here?" St. Peter demanded.

"What's the matter? Don't you let the Irish in?" the man demanded.

"Irish women. But only very special Irish men. What's so special about you?"

"Well," the man said, "I guess not too much. Except one thing—I was the first Catholic boy to marry a Protestant girl in Belfast."

"That is special," St. Peter said. "And when did the wedding take place?"

"About five minutes ago," the Irishman said.

Two big, tough guys wearing masks and with big bulges under their jackets walked into a Dublin pub and said, "Gentlemen, it's time for all good Irishmen to make their annual contributions to the Irish Republican Army. And you'd better dig deep."

The two then walked along the bar taking every cent each patron had. As they approached the end of the bar, Paddy turned to his friend Mick and said, "Here's that five pounds I've owed you since last year."

A newspaper reporter from a U.S. network was interviewing a Belfast resident. "How bad is the killing this year?" the reporter asked.

"Oh, bad, very bad," the Irishman replied. "Why, there's people died this year that have never died before."

What's the difference between a dead dog and a dead Protestant on a Belfast road?
There's skid marks in front of the dog.

CHAPTER 6

GREAT JOKES ABOUT IRISH CHILDREN

Mrs. McGuire was driving down the street with twelve children in her station wagon. A cop parked by the side of the road watched her zip right through a stop sign. He chased her, put on his flashers, and pulled her over. When he went up to her window, he asked, "Lady, don't you know when to stop?"

She pointed to the children in the backseat and said, "Officer, two of them aren't mine."

How did the Irish kid get back at his teacher?
He brought her an apple one morning, then turned her in for receiving stolen property.

Did you hear about the Irish kid who did a great bird imitation?
He ate worms.

Why do they frisk for weapons outside an Irish school?
If you don't have one, they give you one.

Why do they hold Irish elementary-school graduation parties at a soccer stadium?
So the graduates can bring their wives and kids.

What happens when an Irish kid takes a sick day from school?
The teacher sends a thank-you note home.

Why don't Irish kids play hide-and-seek?
Who would come looking for them?

Young Ryan O'Bourke attended a horse auction with his father. He watched as his father moved from horse to horse, running his hands up and down the horses' legs, rump, and chest. After a few minutes Ryan asked, "Pop, why are you doing that?"

"Because I'm thinking of buying these horses."

Ryan looked worried. "Then I think we'd better hurry home right away."

"Why?" his father asked.

"Because the milkman came by yesterday, and I think he wants to buy Ma."

An eight-year-old Irish kid walked into a pub, stepped up to the bar, and said to the barmaid, "Give me a double whiskey."

She looked at him and said, "What do you want to do, get me into trouble?"

"Maybe later," the kid said. "But for now, just give me the whiskey."

Mr. O'Malley came home from work one day to see his son Sean riding down the street on a brand-new ten-speed bicycle. He went up to the boy and said, "How dare you steal a new bike?"

The boy said, "I didn't steal this, I bought it."

The father glowered. "It must have cost three hundred bucks. How could you get that kind of money?"

"I earned it by hiking."

Mr. O'Malley was confused. "You must be lying to me. How could you earn that kind of money by hiking?"

"Easy," the boy said, "Twice a week Mr. Riley the postman comes in the house to see Mommy. Then he gives me twenty dollars to take a hike."

Why didn't the Irish farm lad want to bring his girlfriend to the dance?
She was Bossie.

The school psychologist said, "Mrs. Murphy, I think you're overreacting. Masturbation is normal for a boy your son's age. Many boys masturbate."

"I know," Mrs. Murphy replied. "But not in church."

Sister Francis Mary asked the sixth graders, "Who made you?"

Ryan replied, "The angels."

Sean replied, "God."

Maureen replied, "You mean, lately?"

The nun was conducting a religious class when she asked little Patrick, "Where does Jesus live?"

The Irish lad thought for a moment, then replied, "He lives in our bathroom."

The shocked nun said, "What makes you think that?"

Patrick replied, "Every morning Pa wakes up, kicks the bathroom door, and shouts, 'Christ, are you still in there?' "

Little Sean was lonely growing up on a rural Irish farm. One day his father came home from market leading a little lamb. He came up to the boy and said, "Son, this lamb is yours."

Sean was ecstatic. He named the lamb Sonny, and they became inseparable friends, spending day after day romping over the fields. One day, however, Sonny wandered onto the train tracks and before Sean could react, was hit by a train.

Sean ran to get his father, then returned to find the lamb lying motionless by the tracks. The boy was inconsolable. Finally his father said, "Sean, we have a custom here in Ireland called the wake.

On the day we bury your Sonny, we'll call in all the neighbors. Your ma and the other ladies will bake cakes and pies, and make fresh cream and ice cream. Then we'll have party hats and favors, and we'll play music and sing and dance all night."

Sean was about to respond when, miraculously, the lamb stirred, then struggled groggily to his feet. Sean turned to his father and said, "Pa, what are you waiting for? Kill that lamb."

The Irish mother was talking to her little seven-year-old lass. She said, "You're only a girl now. But someday you'll grow up to meet a man who is handsome, charming, and kind. You'll take long walks through the countryside, have deep talks about music and literature, gaze together at the magnificent works of art in museums, and share a passion for theater. You will have a true marriage of the minds. Do you want that?"

"I think so, Mommy," the little girl said. "But is it really better than screwing?"

The kid walked into the living room and asked, "Dad, can I have five dollars to buy a guinea pig?"

His father said, "Son, here's ten dollars. Go find yourself a nice Irish girl."

The priest was visiting the Irish family when little Ryan walked in and announced, "Ma, I gotta pee." Embarrassed, the mother took the tot aside and said, "It isn't polite to say 'pee.' From now on, when you have to go, say that you have to 'whisper.' "

The little boy nodded. In the middle of the night, the boy came into his parents' bedroom, shook his father, and said, "I gotta whisper."

The groggy father said, "Go whisper in your mother's ear."

Young Patrick O'Toole was hauled before the principal for sipping whiskey during recess. The irate young Irish lad demanded, "Who ratted on me?"

The principal said, "A little bird told me."

"You can't trust anyone," Patrick replied. "And I've been feeding the little bastards every day."

A woman visitor gave an orange to little Ryan O'Toole. His mother said, "Now, what do you say to the nice lady?"

He replied, "Peel it."

An Irish teacher asked the class, "Children, what do you call the person who tells a pilot where to land?"

Little Ryan said, "Now, that would be the hijacker."

The teacher was surprised when little Bridget handed her an apple in the morning. "Thank you, my dear," she said. "But every morning for four months you've handed me a bag of raisins. Why the change?"

Bridget said, " 'Cause the rabbit died."

"Sean, if your father earned four hundred dollars a week and he gave your mother half, what would she have?"

The little Irish boy replied, "A heart attack."

Eamonn Ryan was sitting in the classroom, crying. When the teacher asked what was wrong, he replied, "I just learned I have to stay in this dumb school until I'm eighteen."

The teacher started to cry. "I have to stay here until I'm sixty-five."

The little Irish lad came up to the teacher and asked, "Mrs. Shannon, would you ever punish me for something I didn't do?"

"Of course not."

"Good. Because I didn't do my homework."

The teacher asked, "What are the three words used most frequently by boys and girls?"

Little Sean said, "I don't know."

"That's the first correct answer you've given in months."

The little Irish boy came home from his first day of school and said, "I hate this."

His mother asked, "Why?"

"I can't read, I can't write, and the teacher won't let me talk."

Little Maureen told her mother, "I wish I'd been born a hundred years ago."

"Why?"

"Because you wouldn't dare tell a little old lady to clean up her room."

One Irish lad asked another, "I wonder why babies cry so much?"

His friend replied, "Because they're too young to swear."

Ryan went up to his father and said, "Pop, if you give me a dollar, I'll tell you what the milkman said to Mama this morning."

The suddenly concerned father forked over the dollar, then said, "Well, what did he say?"

"He said, 'We've got a special on sour cream this week.' "

The mother said, "Sean, if you don't go to school, they'll send me and your dad to jail."
"Oh," he replied. "For how long?"

What note did the Irish mother pin to her son's chest before he went to church school?
"The opinions of this child regarding the Bible and God do not necessarily reflect those of his family."

Did you hear about the Irish kid who was born at home?
When his mother saw him, she went to the hospital.

CHAPTER 7

GREAT JOKES ABOUT IRISH SENIOR CITIZENS

What do Irish spinsters wear in their lockets?
A picture of a candle.

A salesman was staying in an Irish inn where
the bathrooms were down the hall. He awoke
before dawn with a full bladder.

He didn't have a bathrobe, so he chanced a
naked dash to the bathroom. But halfway down
the hall, a door opened and three old maids came
out of their room.

The salesman froze like a statue. The first old
maid looked at him and put a nickel in his
mouth. The second old maid put a dime in his
mouth. The third old maid put a quarter in his
mouth and grabbed his penis. "Look," she told
her friends, "it dispenses hand lotion!"

The Irish spinster was given a surprise birthday
party by her nieces and nephews. They brought
in the blazing birthday cake. The old maid started
to cut the cake, but a niece stopped her, saying,
"Aunt Martha, you're supposed to make a wish,
blow out the candles, and take them out of the
cake."

"I know," she snapped. "But if I get my wish, I won't need the candles."

What's the most useless thing in an Irish grandma's house?
Grandpa's thing.

The elderly Irish couple were listening to a religious broadcast from the Dublin Cathedral when the cardinal called out, "God will heal you all. Just stand up, put one hand on the radio, and place the other hand on the part of your body that's sick."

The old woman got to her feet, put one hand on the radio and the other on her arthritic hip. The old man put one hand on the radio and the other on his cock.

"Don't be foolish, Paddy," the old woman snapped. "His Holiness said God would heal the sick, not raise the dead!"

Old Sean O'Riley told his wife that it was time to go to town to apply for his old-age pension. His wife said, "You don't have a birth certificate. How are you going to prove how old you are?"

The man told her not to worry. And sure enough, he arrived back home a few hours later with his first check.

"What did you do?" his wife asked him.

"I just unbuttoned my shirt and showed them the gray hairs on my chest," O'Riley said.

His wife grimaced. "Then why didn't you drop your trousers and apply for disability?"

What's the difference between a young Irishman and an old Irishman?
The young don't know what to do, and the old can no longer do what they know.

Mr. O'Rourke, a bookkeeper by profession, lived with his mother for the first sixty-one years of his life. She finally passed away at age eighty-four. Six months later, to the surprise of everyone who knew him, Mr. O'Rourke announced his engagement.

The wedding took place shortly afterward, and the couple went off on their honeymoon. Sean, O'Rourke's neighbor, came over to the house shortly after their return. Curious, he got the very meek and proper bookkeeper aside and whispered, "So, O'Rourke, how did you find it?"

The Irishman blushed, then replied, "With difficulty."

"What do you mean, with difficulty?"

O'Rourke leaned over and whispered, "Who would have thought to look under all that hair?"

Where do most Irish spinsters get their first date?
On their tombstones.

Two old Irish women were sitting on the bench talking when one asked the other, "How's your Paddy holding up in bed these days?"

The second old woman replied, "He makes me feel like an exercise bike."

"How's that?"

"He climbs on and starts pumping away, but we never get anywhere."

What's the definition of a fussy Irish spinster?
Someone who peels her cucumbers before sitting on them.

How can you tell an Irish spinster's been using cucumbers?
When the salad comes, so does she.

What's a garden-variety romance?
An Irish spinster who uses a cucumber and a carrot.

What's an Irish spinster?
A do-it-yourself expert.

How can you tell you're in an Irish spinster's bathroom?
The plunger's inside the toilet.

Two old Irishmen were sitting in the pub when one hoisted his pint and proclaimed, "Here's to old Paddy. He died for his beliefs."
"What did he believe?" the second one asked.
"He believed that at sixty, he could drink like a twenty-year-old."

Old farmer O'Reilly got drunk one night and no one could find him. They looked everywhere —behind the barn, in the hayloft, but he was nowhere in sight. Finally the hired hand heard the sows snorting and went to check. There was O'Reilly, lying in the mud with an old sow and stroking her belly. The hired hand heard him mutter, "Grandma, I've been sleeping with you for forty years, and this is the first time I noticed your nightgown has two rows of buttons."

An old Irishman tottered into a pub, sat down at the bar, and said to the bartender, "I'd like a shot of whiskey and two drops of water."
The bartender's eyebrows lifted a bit, but he served as requested.
A few minutes later, the old codger again said,

"I'd like a shot of whiskey and two drops of water."

The bartender served him, then watched. Finally, after a fifth request, he couldn't help asking, "Sir, I understand your taste for whiskey. But why the two drops of water?"

The old Irishman said, "When you get to my age, you know your limitations. I can hold my liquor, but I can't hold my water."

An Irish TV reporter was interviewing Eamonn O'Toole on his hundredth birthday. "Tell me, Mr. O'Toole," the reporter began, "you must have seen a lot of changes during your lifetime."

"You got that right, sonny," the feisty centenarian replied. "And I've been against all of them."

An old Irishman hobbled into the brothel and told the madam, "I want a young girl."

She said, "Are you sure, Pop? You must be ninety."

"Ninety-two last week," he said proudly.

"Then you've had it."

The old codger looked puzzled. "I have? Well, then, how much do I owe?"

The hotel manager received an angry call from an Irish spinster in room 659. She shouted, "There's a pervert in the room across the courtyard. He's got the shades down, and he's walking back and forth across the room totally naked."

The manager immediately went up, knocked on the door, walked into the room, and went to the window. He looked for a moment, then said, "Madam, he does have the shades down. But all I can see is his head."

The Irish spinster barked, "You have to put the desk chair on the bed and stand on it."

An elderly Irishman boarded a train, carrying a huge suitcase. A few minutes later, the conductor came around and asked him where he was going.

"Dublin," the Irishman replied.

"That will be twenty pounds," the conductor said.

"Twenty pounds!" the Irishman roared. "Why, that's robbery. I never pay more than ten."

"Well, the fare is twenty now, so pay up."

"I'll pay ten and not a shilling more."

"Twenty," the conductor demanded.

"Ten."

"Twenty."

"Ten."

The conductor was furious now. He noticed that the train was passing over a wide river, so he pointed at the valise and threatened, "If you don't give me twenty pounds right now, I'll throw this bag into the river."

The Irishman's face turned bright red. "I should have known. You're not only trying to rob me, but now you want to drown my poor innocent grandson."

CHAPTER 8

GREAT JOKES ABOUT IRISH POLITICIANS

Why did everyone look up to the Irish politician?
He was born poor but honest—and he overcame
both those disabilities.

How do Irish fairy tales begin?
"If I am elected . . ."

What song do they play when the Irish politician
enters the room?
"Here Comes the Bribe."

How can you tell an Irish politician is lying?
His lips are moving.

Why do Irish politicians believe in free speech?
Because that's all it's worth.

   The white-haired Irish politician, obviously in
his seventies, paced nervously back and forth
in the hospital waiting room. Finally a nurse came
out and told him that his twenty-four-year-old
wife had just delivered twins.

A huge grin came to the ruddy face of the politician. He puffed out his chest and bragged, "That'll show all my political opponents who laughed when we got married. There may be snow on my roof, but there's still a raging fire in my furnace."

The nurse replied, "There may be a fire, but I'd advice you to clean the soot out of your chimney—both babies are black."

A man came up to a friend on the street and asked, "Who are you going to vote for in the election, O'Malley or Shannahan?"

The second man grimaced. "Who cares? All politicians are the same—they treat us all like mushrooms."

"Mushrooms?"

"Yeah," the second man replied. "They keep us in the dark and feed us nothing but shit."

What do you need when you have three Irish politicians buried up to their necks in cement? More cement.

What's an Irish politician? Someone who can give you his complete attention and not hear a word you say.

A man knelt in the confessional and said, "Father, yesterday I got so mad that I went out and killed an Irish politician."

The priest said, "I don't care about your community-service work. I'm here to listen to your sins."

An Irish politician was campaigning when someone asked, "Do you believe in imbibing alcoholic beverages?"

The politician asked, "Is this an inquisition or an invitation?"

How does an Irish politician spend his days? He spends half his time making laws, and half his time helping his friends evade them.

The Irish politician told his wife, "I've been asked to throw the first ball out at the start of the season next week."

She retorted, "The way you've been lately, you might as well throw them both out."

Why do so many Irish politicians get divorced? They don't take the time to do to their wives what they do to the voters.

The Irish politician called his wife and said, "Darling, I've been elected."

"Honestly?" she replied in surprise.

"Now, don't bring that up."

Why do Irish politicians need three hats?
One to wear, one to toss into the ring, and one to talk through.

How do you know Irish politicians are drunkards? They're always making their speeches from the floor of Parliament.

A little boy was taken by his father to see the Irish Parliament. He watched for a moment, then asked, "Dad, why is that priest there?"

The father said, "He's the chaplain of the Parliament."

"You mean, he prays for the members?"

"No," the father replied. "When he sees how the members behave, he prays for the country."

An Irish politician was hurrying down a country road to another campaign stop when his car slid off into a ditch. He walked a few miles to a farmhouse and persuaded the farmer to bring a horse with him back to the car. The farmer hitched the horse to the car, and the animal pulled it out of the ditch.

The politician, with a big smile, offered the farmer five dollars and a hearty handshake. The politician added, "I hope you'll vote for me on election day."

The farmer grunted, then said, "I feel about you the way that horse does."

The politician looked at the horse. To his amazement, the horse had a huge hard-on. He said, "Why is he like that?"

"Because," the farmer replied, "he knows that all politicians are cocksuckers."

What is usually the last thing an Irish politician runs for?
The border.

Did you hear that Irish politicians believe in doing the greatest good for the greatest number?
And to them, the greatest number is Number One.

What's the political equivalent of a "man bites dog" news story?
"Bull throws Irish politician."

CHAPTER 9

GREAT JOKES ABOUT IRISH MARRIAGES

What do you call an Irish couple's waterbed?
Lake Placid.

What's another name for an Irish couple's marriage bed?
The Dead Sea.

Colleen was sitting on the bus with a friend, who asked, "How's your diet going?"

Colleen grumbled. "I went to that new diet doctor. He told me that every time I make love, I lose three hundred calories."

"That's terrific."

"Not when you're married to Sean. I figure I've lost an average of fifty calories a year."

Two Irish guys were sitting next to each other in a bar. The talk turned to their home life. One guy said to another, "My old lady has a mouth that won't stop. I'd give anything for one day's truce in our household."

The second guy said, "One day isn't anything. My wife and I didn't have a single argument for twenty-seven years."

"That's astounding," the first guy said. "But what happened after twenty-seven years?"

"We met."

What happened on the Irishman's wedding night? His bride told him they were seeing too much of each other.

Colleen said to her friend, "Sex with Paddy is like the Fourth of July."

"You mean, all fireworks and bright lights?"

"No. I mean, it happens once a year."

It started to pour in the middle of the afternoon, so the Irish construction laborer came home early from work. He walked into his bedroom to find the mailman and his wife pumping away on the bed. The Irishman's face got bright red, and he shouted, "What's going on here?"

His wife turned to the mailman and said, "See, I told you he was stupid."

An Irishman met a friend in the pub who asked, "How's it going?" The guy shrugged and said, "Some good news and some bad news. First, the druggist sent my wife cyanide instead of bromide, and she died."

"That's awful."

"No," the guy said, "that's the good news. The bad news is he's charging me an extra ten bucks."

The Irish newlyweds arrived at their honeymoon cottage and didn't stir from the room for nearly twenty-four hours. When they finally left the bedroom, the husband went down to the local pub to order dinner.

When he returned to the room, his bride uncovered one dish. The groom said, "That corned beef and cabbage is mine."

She took the other plate, uncovered it, and was shocked to see only a head of lettuce on the plate.

"What's this?" she asked her husband.

"I want to see if you eat like a rabbit, too."

An Irishman was drinking at a bar. His friend came up and asked what was happening. The man replied, "Well, last night my wife came home and told me she had some good news and some bad news."

"So what did she say?"

"The first thing she told me was that she was running away with the guy who lives next door."

"What did you say to that?"

Paddy took a sip of his drink, then replied, "I asked her what the bad news was."

Paddy and Sean were closing a bar one night when one said to the other, "God, I hate going home at this hour. All I want to do is sneak in and drop into bed, but my wife wakes up and nags the shit out of me for hours."

"You're doing it all wrong, trying to sneak in," Sean said. "I stomp in, slam the door, and scream out, 'Okay, darling, let's fuck!' My wife always pretends to be asleep."

Mrs. O'Brady was gossiping with a friend. "You know," she whispered, "I heard that Colleen was pregnant when she was married. Is that true?"

"Well," Mrs. O'Sullivan replied, "they did throw puffed rice at her wedding."

The pub keeper approached a very tipsy Mr. O'Neal sitting at the bar and asked, "Is there anything the matter? You've been belting them down hard for hours."

"My wife died yesterday," the Irishman said.

"I'm sorry," the pub keeper said. "Have a drink on me. It must be hard losing a wife."

O'Neal laughed. "Hard? It was bloody near impossible!"

The mortician was laying out the body of a man with an unbelievably long penis. He called in his Irish receptionist to show her. She took a look, then said, "That's just like my Paddy's.'

The mortician asked, "You mean, he's got one that long?"

"No," she replied. "That dead."

How do you know Irish husbands are really bad in bed?
Their wives go out and take headache lessons.

Paddy visited his parents the day after his wedding. His father took him aside and asked him, "How did it go last night, son?"

Paddy winked and elbowed his dad. "Gee, great. You know, the way she was acting, I think I could have fucked her."

Why is an Irish groom like George Bush?
When he finally gets in, he's got no idea what to do.

The Irishman finally got married, but he had no idea what to do on his wedding night. His exasperated bride finally said, "Look, here's what you do. You take that thing you love to have in your hand and put it where I pee."

So the guy got up and tossed his whiskey bottle in the sink.

Twenty-five-year-old Ryan O'Rourke was still living at home. One day his father came into his room and found him masturbating. "That's it," the father said, "I've got to get you married off."

The father made arrangements for a mail-order bride from the Philippines, and two months later his son was married to pretty little Kwan-Lo. But a week after the wedding, the father walked into his son's house to find the loser beating off. "Are you crazy?" he yelled. "That Kwan-Lo is a wonderful girl."

"I know, Pop," Ryan said. "But her arm gets awful tired sometimes."

One Irishman was downing them faster than usual when the man on the barstool next to him said, "What's wrong?"

The first Irishman said, "I'm drinking to the memory of my wife. She was a saint on earth. She went to church every single morning, spent her days reading and quoting the Scriptures, sang hymns and psalms all evening, filled our house with religious statues and paintings, and invited priests and nuns to dinner three times a week."

"She sounds perfect," the second man commented. "How did a pious woman come to die so young?"

The first Irishman replied, "I strangled her."

An Irishman saved for years for his first trip to New York City. He arrived at the airport, took the bus to his hotel, and checked in at the desk. The clerk was very patient with the very naive Paddy, repeating five times the directions to something called an "elevator." As the Irishman ambled in that direction, he saw a very fat, very ugly old lady standing in front of a door. To his surprise, the door opened, the fat lady waddled inside, then the door closed.

Fascinated, the Irishman waited patiently for the door to open again. When it did, a gorgeous young blonde sauntered out. "Begorrah!" the Irishman exclaimed. "I knew I should have brought my wife!"

One Irishman said to another, "You know, my wife's the greatest cook in the world."

"How do you know?"

"Every night when I come home, there's a half dozen truck drivers eating in the kitchen."

What three things can the average Irish husband do in three minutes?
Drain a can of beer, belch, and make love to his wife.

What do you call an Irish wife who moans and shudders and cries out during sex?
A hypocrite.

A very intoxicated Irishman came staggering into the police station one night and announced,

"I pushed my wife down a flight of stairs. Throw me in jail."

The desk sergeant asked, "Did you kill her?"

"I don't think so," the drunk replied. "That's why I want you to throw me in jail."

"I was in bed last night," a woman confided to her friend, "when Paddy came home from the bar. He climbed in and started running his hand up and down my leg. I started to feel that old familiar sensation."

"Arousal?" the friend asked.

"Headache."

How did the Irishman know his marriage was in trouble?
His wife's favorite sex aid was Pepto-Bismal.

Mrs. O'Malley, all dressed in black, was standing by the coffin of her recently deceased husband. A neighbor lady came up, gazed at the departed, then remarked, "He looks so peaceful lying there. I trust he didn't suffer before the end."

"My poor Paddy," Mrs. O'Malley said. "He had a terrible time, dying of syphilis."

"My goodness!" the woman exclaimed. She crossed herself and moved on.

Then Mrs. O'Malley's son came up and said, "Ma, what a terrible thing to say about Da. You know he died of diarrhea."

"I know," the Irish widow said. "But I want people to think he died being a sport, rather than the shit he was all his life."

Mick O'Reilly was sitting at the end of the bar looking grim when a friend asked, "Mick, what's wrong? You look terrible."

"It's my wife," O'Reilly said. "I came home drunk one night, and she said she wouldn't talk to me for a month."

"That's awful."

"You've said a mouthful," O'Reilly said. "Today's the last day of that month."

Mrs. Hoolihan went up to her husband and said, "My dear mother is now dead and gone. What kind of tombstone should we get her?"

Hoolihan grimaced. "A heavy one."

Mrs. O'Toole walked into the gun shop and said, "I'd like a revolver for my husband."

"Certainly, madam," the owner replied. "What model would he like?"

"He doesn't have a preference," Mrs. O'Toole replied. "He doesn't even know I'm going to shoot him."

Two months after the wedding, the new bride went to the doctor and complained, "Every night I dress in a slinky nightgown and cuddle up to my husband. But every night he falls asleep in thirty seconds. What can I do?"

The doctor reached for a bottle of pills, grabbed a pencil, and said, "These pills will solve the problem. Have him take one with dinner every night. Now, what's his name?"

"Paddy O'Shea."

The doctor groaned, "Ah, an Irishman." He grabbed a second bottle, handed it to the woman, and said, "You take one of these before bed every night."

She was puzzled, "How can I get him interested in sex by taking a pill?"

The doctor said, "That's impossible. But now you'll fall asleep too."

One Irish wife asked another, "Was your Patrick a bit shy when you got married?"

"I'll say," the second wife replied. "If he hadn't been, our son would be five years old."

Maureen O'Shea had a very severe heart attack. Her husband rushed to the hospital to find her in critical condition. The doctor took him aside and said, "Your wife will be dead in a couple of hours if she doesn't get a heart transplant. Unfortunately, no suitable human donors are available. However, we've been testing a method of transplanting the heart of a cow into a human being. It's very risky, but your wife faces certain death."

The idea of his wife having a cow's heart shocked O'Shea, but he finally realized he had no choice. He consented to the operation. To his surprise and delight, his wife survived the operation and recovered quickly. A month later, she went home.

Two weeks later, the doctor called the Irishman in and asked how his wife was making out. The man replied, "Well, I guess I'd say good and bad."

"What do you mean?"

"On the plus side," the man replied, "her grazing keeps the grass nice and short. The embarrassing thing is that she goes door to door every morning breast-feeding the neighborhood."

The Irishman was passing out cigars on the construction site to celebrate the birth of his son. Someone asked, "How much did the kid weigh?"

"Four pounds," said the proud father.

"That's small."

"What do you expect?" the Irishman said belligerently. "We've only been married three months."

The Irish woman was admiring herself in the mirror. She said, "You know, I still look the same as I did on our wedding day."

Another woman said, "Well, there is one slight difference."

"What?"

"You're not pregnant."

After six years of marriage, Paddy's wife was increasingly upset that her husband insisted on making love in total darkness. Finally, determined to overcome his shyness, she flipped the light on one night. To her utter amazement, he was screwing her with a dildo in his hand.

"You impotent bastard," she swore. "How dare you fool me like that for six years? You'd better explain yourself."

"I'll be glad to," he replied. "If you'll explain our three kids."

An Irish girl finally got her fiancé to the altar two weeks before Easter. On their wedding night she got into a short, sexy nightgown, crawled into bed, and started caressing her husband. But he didn't respond.

"What's wrong?" she asked.

"I . . . I can't make love," he stammered. "It's Lent."

"Lent?" she roared. "To whom and for how long?"

Why did the Irish wife think her husband was unfaithful?

None of the children looked like him.

A man hadn't seen his friend O'Reilly for a few months, so he asked, "How's your new bride?"

O'Reilly grimaced. "I'm afraid I married a nymphomaniac. Two weeks ago, we went to see a three-piece combo at a bar, and the next night I caught her in bed with the three musicians. Last week, we went to a basketball game, and the next night I caught her in bed with all five guys on the starting team."

"That's terrible."

"You haven't heard anything yet," O'Reilly said. "Tomorrow is the St. Patrick's Day parade."

Maureen walked into the kitchen and said to Paddy, "What would it take for you to go on a second honeymoon?"

"A second wife," he replied.

Patrick O'Malley fell to his death from the top floor of the construction project. His widow got the check from his company insurance. But shortly afterward she was besieged by creditors, the landlord, tax collectors, lawyers, and the like.

One day she was sitting at the kitchen table surrounded by paperwork. When a neighbor walked in and asked how she was doing, she replied, "It's a terrible burden. You know, every once in a while I find myself wishing O'Malley hadn't fallen."

On the first night of their honeymoon, Eileen turned to Patrick and said, "I'm afraid I have a confession to make. Before we met, I used to be a topless dancer."

Shocked, the Irishman replied, "Why, you might as well have told me you were a whore."

She said, "Uh, there is one more thing I have to confess . . ."

Did you hear about the lazy Irishman?
He bought his wife a vibrator and told her to buzz off.

O'Reilly was off to the city to sell his crop. The first buyer he found bought everything, so he wired his wife he'd be back a day early. When he arrived, he walked into his bedroom, saw his hired hand screwing his wife, and stormed out of the house. The next day, he was walking into church when he ran into his mother-in-law. He told her, "I'm telling Father McMurphy that I'm divorcing that whoring daughter of yours."

"Not so fast," she said. "I know Doreen wouldn't do something like that without a good reason. After all these years, give me a chance to find out what it was."

O'Reilly agreed. The next day, he met his mother-in-law on the steps of the church. She beamed and said, "I just knew Doreen had a good reason."

"And what was it?"

"She never got your telegram."

What's the surest sign an Irishman is in love?
When he divorces his wife.

Why is a typical Irish husband like a Christmas tree?
They both have balls for decoration.

An Irishman went off to New York to visit relatives. He was appalled by the big city. People rudely pushed by him, he gawked in amazement at the sky-high prices in the store, and he reacted with horror when the bartender at the pub charged him five dollars for a drink. When his cousin met him, he complained, "I don't know how you live here. This is an awful place. Give me Dublin anytime."

"And why is Dublin so great?" his cousin asked.

"Why, every time a body visits Dublin, you get all you can drink for free, sleep in a fancy hotel without paying a cent, and wake up to find fifty dollars on your dresser."

"Come on," the cousin said. "I don't believe that. Did it ever happen to you?"

"Well, no," the Irishman said. "But it happens to my wife all the time."

The Irish couple walked into a bar. The wife looked around, then said to her husband, "You see that man downing one drink after another at the end of the bar? That's O'Malley, and he's been drinking like that since I jilted him ten years ago."

The husband said, "That's ridiculous. I don't care how good the reason, ten years is too long to celebrate."

The Irish newlyweds arrived at their honeymoon cottage. She went into the bathroom first, then emerged wearing only a towel. He pulled out the camera, then said, "Honey, please drop the towel. I want to take a picture of you nude to carry with me always."

She complied, and he took his snapshot. Then he went into the bathroom and emerged a few minutes later wearing just a towel. She said, "Well, drop it so I can get a look."

He dropped the towel. She looked for a moment, then grabbed the camera. He said, "Are you taking that picture so you can carry it with you always?"

"No," she replied. "I want to get it enlarged."

A tourist was standing on the streets of Dublin when a funeral procession appeared. Walking right behind the coffin was a man holding an Irish setter on a leash. Following him was the longest line of mourners the tourist had ever seen. He watched in amazement for a moment, then asked one of the men in the procession, "Who is this funeral for?"

The man replied, "Why, it's for the mother-in-law of Patrick Murphy. That Irish setter of his suddenly attacked and killed her."

"That's awful," the tourist said. Then he added, "Say, do you think there's any chance Murphy would lend me that dog?"

The man gestured behind him. "What do you think we're all in line for?"

On his wedding night, the Irish bridegroom got down on his knees. His bride asked, "What are you doing?"

"I'm praying for guidance."

She took his hand. "I'll take care of the guidance. You pray for endurance."

The Irish couple was sitting in the marriage counselor's office when the husband said, "I like sex just as much as the next man. But this nymphomaniac wants it three or four times a year!"

What did the Irishman do when his wife told him she'd dance on his grave?
Arranged a burial at sea.

An Irishman was working on his fourth pint when a funeral procession came down the street outside the pub. The Irishman put down his glass, stood up, took off his cap, and held it over his heart until the procession passed.

The bartender said, "Paddy, that was very thoughtful."

The Irishman shrugged. "It's the least I could do. After all, we were married thirty-one years."

The Irishman walked into the bar one night with a big grin on his face and ordered a round of drinks for the house. A buddy asked, "Why are you so happy?"

"Well, last night I got home early, walked into the bedroom, and found her in the sack with three guys."

The guy said, "How in the hell could that make you happy?"

Paddy said, "When I asked her what she was doing, she said, 'I told you no one man could take your place.' "

The Irishman walked into a neighborhood bar and a neighbor called, "Hey, Reilly, you idiot. You gotta pull down the shades when you're humping your old lady—I could see everything."

Reilly got a big grin on his face. "You're wrong, Kearney. The joke's on you. I wasn't even home last night."

Why did the Irish wife put a car battery on her husband's side of the bed?
Because she could never get him started.

The Irish couple had thirteen kids and a host of other troubles, but somehow the wife had managed to keep the family fed, clothed, and intact. On their twenty-fifth wedding anniversary, the couple was given a gala party at the local pub by their friends and relatives. There was much eating, drinking, and rejoicing. Finally, at the end of the party, the Irishman climbed up on a table and shouted, "We can't end this party without a final tribute to the one true, wonderful, caring person who made my life worth living all of these long twenty-five years. I love her dearly." As the crowd cheered, he jumped down off the table and embraced the pubkeeper.

An Irishman's beloved wife died, and friends and relatives came from miles around for the traditional lively Irish wake. The next morning, the Irishman was finally awakened by his daughter, who said, "Come on, Da, it's time for Ma's funeral."
The Irishman shook some cobwebs from his brain, then said, "Run along and tell Father O'Reilly we'll not be having a funeral today. Last night was so much fun I figure we'll keep your ma on ice a couple more days."

An Irishman was sitting in a bar when he said to a friend, "You know, my wife's a saint. Always doing something to help somebody."

"Like what?"

"Like the homeless problem."

The friend asked, "How does she help the homeless?"

The Irishman replied, "When I got home the other night, I found out she'd given her nightgown to the poor and let these two guys live in our closet."

An Irishman was sitting at the bar when a friend said, "Why are you here tonight?"

Paddy replied, "My wife threw me out of the house for being honest."

"How's that?"

"Well, we were watching TV when she asked me, 'What can I do to make you more interested in sex?' And I said, 'Leave town.' "

An Irishman walked into a psychiatrist's office and said, "Doc, I've got a problem. My wife believes that she's a horse."

"Exactly how does this belief manifest itself?" the shrink asked.

"Well," the man said, "she spends all day and all night naked on all fours."

"My goodness," the psychiatrist exclaimed. "That must be embarrassing."

"I'm used to it by now," the Irishman said. "But that's not the real reason I came."

"I know," the shrink said, "you're concerned that she's eating oats and hay."

"No," the husband said. "They're a lot cheaper than steaks and chops."

"I see. But her . . . her bathroom habits embarrass you."

"No. We use the manure in the garden."

"Then what is it that bothers you?" the shrink demanded.

"There's three guys who think they're stallions who hang around every day mounting her. Now she's in foal."

CHAPTER 10

GREAT IRISH SEX JOKES

Why did the Irish newlyweds stay up all night?
They were waiting for their sexual relations to arrive.

What do you call an Irish hooker with spring in her walk?
Tramp O'Leen.

What do Irish men do when they lose interest in sex?
They get married.

Three guys, an Englishman, an Italian, and an Irishman, were sitting at lunch talking about where they were going that night. The Englishman said, "I know this place down by the river where you get every third drink free."

"That's nothing," the Italian said. "My brother-in-law told me about this place that just opened that's giving every other drink free."

The Irishman said, "I know a place in my neighborhood where every drink is free, and at the end of the night you get laid in the parking lot."

"Wow," said his friends. "How did you find out about that place?"

"From my wife," the Irishman replied.

An Irish farmer ran into a friend at the market in their small village. The friend asked, "Where have you been? I haven't seen you in a while."

The farmer said, "I saved enough to go away on vacation."

"Where did you go?"

"To America. To New York City."

The friend was impressed. "That's wonderful. Did you have a good time?"

The Irishman said, "Oh, yes. I spent two weeks in a whorehouse."

The friend remarked, "That must have been very expensive."

"No," the Irishman replied. "They were all my relatives."

Why did the Irish girl have her zip code tatooed on her thighs?
She was dying to get some male in her box.

Why is an Irish girl like a prizefighter?
She won't go into action until she sees a ring.

What happened when the Irishman called the telephone porno service?

The girl said, "Not tonight. I've got an earache."

Did you hear about the Irishman who was arrested after his girlfriend filed a paternity suit?

He was charged with leaving the scene of an accident.

Did you hear about the Irishman with a small dick?

When a girl took his prick in her mouth, she didn't suck, she flossed.

An Irishman met a woman in a bar, bought her many drinks, and ended up back in her apartment. They took off their clothes and hopped in the sack. Afterward, as the guy lit up a cigarette, the girl hopped out of bed and said, "Boy, are you a lousy lover."

The Irishman replied indignantly, "I don't see how you can say that after only two minutes."

Why is an Irish woman's clitoris like Antarctica?

Most Irishmen know it's there, but few really care.

Little Colleen watched her father take a shower. She noticed his testicles and asked him about them. "Those are my apples," he replied.

Quickly the little girl ran into the kitchen and told her mother what Daddy had said. Her mother grimaced and asked, "Did Daddy tell you about the dead limb they were hanging on?"

O'Riley walked into his bedroom to find his wife rolling in the hay with another man. "What in the name of St. Patrick is going on? Who is this man?"

His wife thought for a moment, then said, "That's a fair question." She turned to the guy and said, "What is your name?"

What's the average Irish husband's idea of foreplay?
Warning, "Brace yourself, dear."

Why did God invent booze?
So Irish women would have a chance to get laid.

What's sex with an Irishman like?
Ever try stuffing a marshmallow into a parking meter slot?

How do you describe an Irishman's sex life?
Fist or famine.

Why are Irishmen such lousy lovers?
Because they wait for the swelling to go down.

Why are Irishmen like bumper stickers?
They're both very hard to get off.

The Irish maid's fiancé was home on leave from the army. She was cleaning the kitchen one morning when her employer, Mrs. Reynolds, came in and asked, "Doreen, how long is your young man's furlough?"

Doreen blushed, then replied, "If it please you, ma'am, not as long as Mr. Reynolds'—but it's thicker."

How do we know Irishmen are lazy?
So many of them marry pregnant women.

A single woman who'd gotten very frustrated over her sex life finally confided in her physician. She said, "Doctor, I want to know if there is any way to know how well a man is equipped from his outward appearance."

The doctor said, "The only reliable way is the size of his feet."

The woman thanked the doctor profusely. That night, she went from bar to bar, her eyes firmly fixed to the floor. She'd just about given up when she walked into a seedy corner bar. She spotted a young Irish guy with the largest shoes she'd ever seen. Immediately she went up to him and bought him a bottle of whiskey. By the time he'd finished half the bottle, she'd persuaded him to adjourn to a local hotel.

The next morning, the woman was gone when the Irish guy awoke. He found a twenty-dollar bill on the table, next to a note that read, "Here's twenty dollars. Please go out and buy yourself a pair of shoes that fit."

Colleen had her eye on handsome Patrick McCarthy, and finally she persuaded him to have dinner with her. After a few drinks she led him back to her apartment, where they sat on the couch. As he sipped another drink, she started to nibble his ear and run her hands through his hair.

But all Patrick did was complain about how chilly he was. Desperate, she grew bolder. She unbuttoned her blouse, sat on his lap, and put his hands on her breasts. Nothing seemed to interest him, and he pushed her hands away when she tried to unzip his trousers. Finally she stood up, pulled out the waistband of her panties, pointed, and said, "You know, I've got a hole down there."

He said, "So that's where the draft is coming from."

Why do hookers like turning a trick with an Irishman?
It's a soft job.

Why is an Irishman like a rodeo rider?
They only stay on for eight seconds.

Why is a microwave like an Irishman?
They both heat up instantly, then go "ding" in twenty seconds.

What's the most common four-letter word an Irishman screams during sex?
H-E-L-P.

Why is an Irish lover like the post office?
He takes five days to deliver.

Why is Irish sex like Irish football?
They're both male spectator sports.

What did Mrs. O'Malley give her husband when their tenth child was born?
A stop sign.

An English landowner and his Irish manservant ran into each other in hell one day. "My lord," the Irishman exclaimed. "What are you doing here?"

The landowner sighed. "I'm here because I lied, cheated, and stole to pay the debts run up by that playboy son of mine. But you were a faithful, loyal servant. Why are you here?"

"For fathering that playboy son," the Irishman replied.

Why aren't there any Irish bisexuals?
Twice a year is too much for them.

What's an Irish porno film?
Sixty seconds of sex and fifty-nine minutes of whiskey commercials.

What's the only official Irish birth control?
Kicking your husband in the shins to make him limp.

What did the Irishman say when he saw his best friend on top of his wife?
"Down, Rover."

What's another name for the rhythm method of birth control?
Irish roulette.

Why are the Super Bowl champs like an Irish bridegroom?
They're both on top for a year.

Desperate for a job, a Dublin man took a job on a sheep farm in a remote Irish county.
The work was hard and the social life nonexistent. Finally, after two solid weeks of labor, the foreman announced that a wagon load of beer would be available that evening.

The man wanted female company more than a drink, but one beer led to another. Soon everything was a blur. The next thing he knew, another farmhand was shaking him awake. When he tried to move, he realized he'd never felt worse in his life. His head was pounding, he stank to high heaven, and his dick was so sore he couldn't touch it.

"Come on," the other hand said, "it's time to tend the sheep."

"Fuck the sheep," the man said crossly.

"No, not now," the other hand said. "Didn't you fuck enough of them last night?"

Why is it ridiculous that Irish women complain their husbands make love too fast?
How much speed can you build up in forty-five seconds?

Why did the Irish wife call her husband "filet"?
Because he had practically no bone.

A man walked into a talent agency one day and opened a suitcase. Out popped a tiny man, who sat down at a miniature grand piano and played a brilliant solo.

"Amazing," the agent said. "Where did you get him?"

"Well," the man said. "I was walking through the fields in Ireland one day and I spotted a leprechaun, who told me I was granted one wish."

"And this was your one wish?"

"Not exactly," the man said. "The leprechaun was hard of hearing. So I ended up with a twelve-inch pianist."

How do we know that Adam was Irish?
Who else would have stood next to a naked woman and munched on an apple?

An Irish sailor went into a whorehouse, paid his twenty dollars, and went upstairs with a girl. About fifteen minutes later, he asked, "How am I doing?"

The whore replied, "Oh, about three knots."

"What do you mean, three knots?" the sailor asked.

She said, "You're not hard, you're not in, and you're not getting your money back."

The Irish couple were necking in the living room. "What are you thinking about?" Maureen moaned.

"The same thing you are," Ryan replied. Then he got up, dashed to the refrigerator, and opened two beers.

It was a long night at the bar, and McMurphy was staggering out with a couple of single buddies, who were razzing him about what he'd face when he got home. "Nonsense," McMurphy retorted. "I'll walk in the door, wake her up, rip off her nightgown, put it in her, and everything will be okay."

Sure enough, the Irishman walked in his front door, turned on the light in his bedroom, ripped off his wife's nightgown, and started to climb on top. "Not so fast," she called. "You owe me a good one."

So he started to kiss her. He kissed her on both

ears, on her nose, on her mouth. Then he kissed her shoulders, her breasts, and her belly button. Next he kissed each knee. Then she interrupted, "Hey! If that had been a bar, you wouldn't have passed it up."

Sean O'Malley was working as a laborer on a big construction project. One day the boss's daughter came by, and it was love at first sight. They kept the romance a secret, until one day O'Malley went to see the boss and asked for his daughter's hand.

The arrogant owner retorted, "Why, you only make two hundred dollars a week. That won't keep my daughter in toilet paper."

O'Malley replied, "If she shits that much, forget about it."

Did you hear about the new Irish abortion clinic? The catch is you have to wait twelve months.

The young Irish couple was at the doctor's for their prenuptual physicals. At the end the doctor called the prospective groom in and said, "I'm afraid I have some good news and some bad news."

The young man grimaced. "What's the bad news?"

"Your fiancée has syphilis."

"Oh, no!" he cried. "What could be the good news?"

"She didn't get it from you."

Mrs. Shaughnessy went to the doctor and said, "Doc, Paddy hasn't been able to get it up for years, and I'm desperate. Do you have anything I can give him?"

The doctor said he did, and he wrote out a prescription. Unfortunately, he made a slight error—instead of "2 teaspoons" he wrote "20 teaspoons."

The next evening, Mrs. Shaughnessy dashed into the office and demanded to see the doctor. The physician came out and asked, "What's wrong? Didn't it work?"

"I'll say it worked," the Irish wife replied. "But now I need the antidote so they can close the coffin."

Why did the Irishman put a dime in his condom?
If he could't come, he could call.

Why did the Irishman spend all night outside the whorehouse?
He was waiting for the red light to turn green.

What do you call a handsome, well-endowed guy who can screw all night in Ireland?
A tourist.

The Irish guy climbed on top. A minute later he complained, "Hey, you don't have any tits and your cunt's way too tight."
The woman yelled, "Get off my back."

The Irish couple were making out when the girl moaned, "Oh, please, kiss me where it smells."
So he drove to the dump.

A young Irishman went to a whorehouse for the first time. When he told the madame he was a virgin, she showed him how to put on a rubber, rolling it down his thumb. Then he went upstairs. After he screwed his girl, she said, "That rubber must have broken. I feel wet inside."
The Irishman held up his thumb and said, "No, it didn't. It's as good as new."

The Irish lad was warned by his puritan mother never to have sex with a woman because women's vaginas had teeth that would bite his penis off.
Years went by, the mother passed away, and the Irishman was persuaded to get married. But on his honeymoon night he went into the

bathroom and refused to come out. His bride pleaded, but he said, "No. You've got teeth down there."

"Don't be silly," she said. "Come take a look."

So he opened the door, came over to the bed, inspected her crotch, and stood up. She said, "See, no teeth."

He replied, "Well, with gums like that, no wonder you lost them."

What do you call an Irish couple who use the rhythm method of birth control?
Parents.

An Irishman walked into a bar and ordered twelve shots of whiskey. He made the bartender line them up in front of him, then he downed them one after another.

When he was through, the bartender asked, "Are you celebrating something?"

"My first blow job," the Irishman replied.

The bartender said, "In that case, have another one on me."

The Irishman said, "No, thanks. If twelve won't get the taste out of my mouth, another one won't."

The young Irishman strutted onto the construction site one day and loudly bragged, "Guys, my wife is pregnant."

One of his co-workers snapped, "Who do you suspect?"

How can you tell an Irishman at an orgy?
He's the one saying, "My turn again?"

What happened to the Irishman who was accused of indecent exposure?
They brought him in, stripped him, then released him for insufficient evidence.

What did the Irishman do when a bee stung him on the cock?
Asked the doctor to take away the pain but leave the swelling.

What happened when the Irishman was arrested for flashing?
They tried him in small-claims court.

An Irishman came home to find his daughter and her boyfriend screwing on the couch. He muttered, "Well, I never . . ."

She said, "Daddy, you must have."

Why don't you ever see any women in the Irish Social Club?
The club has no active members.

An Irishman staggered out of the pub and down the street. He stopped when he saw a little boy sitting on the corner, crying. "What's wrong, lad?" he asked.

The boy said, "I'm crying because I can't do what the big boys can do."

So the drunk sat next to him and began to cry.

How can you tell if a playwright is Irish?
He never gets beyond the first act.

Two professors were talking one evening. One said, "I just translated an old Irish myth that might interest you. It said that in the beginning of time, men and women were built exactly alike, and they complained of having nothing to do. So the gods sent an elf to hide under a bridge with a golden hatchet, and he was instructed to gash every other person that walked overhead. Of course, some people were tall, and the elf had to reach high, so they only got small gashes. Some people were the right height, and they got perfect gashes, while short people really got split."

The other professor exclaimed, "That explains

it. My wife must have scooted across the bridge on her ass."

How can you tell Irish girls are really flat?
They have the word "front" tattooed on their chests.

How flat are Irish women?
They have to breast-feed through a straw.

How flat are Irish woman?
When you look down their dresses, the biggest things you see are their corns.

How can you tell an Irish girl is desperate?
She sends change-of-address cards to Peeping Toms.

How ugly are Irish woman?
They look like they ran out of money halfway through a sex-change operation.

Where do Irish woman go for checkups?
The vet.

Why do Irish women love the racetrack?
They're all nags.

How long does it take an Irish girl to finish school?
From now to maternity.

The good Mrs. Shannon came to mass as usual one morning, knelt in front of the altar, and said, "Dear God. I don't understand what's going on. My neighbor, that harlot O'Riley, has been married five times, entertains half the parish in her bedroom, and drinks like a fish, but she's got a huge house, diamonds, and a fancy car. Why has she been so blessed when I haven't?"

Suddenly the face of God appeared above the altar and boomed, "Because she doesn't bug me."

What's the only thing that prevents Irish women from being colorless?
Varicose veins.

What do Irish woman use for birth control?
Their faces.

Why isn't there any prostitution in Ireland?
Irish woman can't even give it away.

How do you tell if a woman is half Irish and half Italian?
She mashes potatoes with her feet.

What happens to Irish girls that look for trouble?
They usually end up with a belly full.

What's the difference between garbage and an Irish girl?
Garbage gets picked up.

Two Irish women met at the market. One said to the other, "Did you hear that Eileen finally got married?"

"Married?" the other replied. "Why, I didn't even know she was pregnant."

The Irish girl knelt in the confessional and said, "Bless me, Father, for I have sinned."

"What is it, child?"

The girl said, "Father, I have committed the sin of vanity. Twice a day I gaze at myself in the mirror and tell myself how beautiful I am."

The priest turned, took a good look at the girl, and said, "My dear, I have good news. That isn't a sin—it's only a mistake."

Mrs. McCarthy walked into the fortune teller's chamber and sat in front of the crystal ball. The seer peered for a few minutes, then said, "I see . . . I see that you are a widow. Prepare yourself for your husband to die a violent death."

"Oh, dear," Mrs. McCarthy exclaimed. "Can you tell me—will I be acquitted?"

Mrs. Shaughnessy arrived in Dublin from the country. Outside the bus station, she hailed a taxi and gave him the address of her sister's house. The driver gunned the motor, then raced off through traffic as if he had a swarm of Protestants chasing him. Mrs. Shaughnessy hung on for dear life as they sped down narrow streets and skidded around the corners. Finally she could hold her tongue no more.

She said, "Driver, be careful. I have nine children at home who need me."

The driver snapped, "Lady, you got nine kids and you're telling me to be careful?"

Sean O'Casey had dated many a lass, but he finally became entranced by Maureen O'Riley. He wooed her and pursued her, but she would not give in and go to bed with him. Finally he proposed marriage and she accepted.

The wedding festivities were gala. That night, as they undressed in their honeymoon cottage, O'Casey said, "You know, Maureen, I never would have wed you if you had gone to bed with me like all the other girls did."

"Experience is the best teacher," Maureen said. "That's how I lost all of my other suitors."

Did you hear about the religious Irish bride? She wouldn't screw in any week that had a Sunday in it.

There was a knock on the front door. When Mrs. McCarthy shouted, "Who's there?", a voice replied, "I've got some very bad news. Paddy's been killed."

"Oh, no," she cried. "How did it happen?"

"I'm afraid he was run over by a steamroller."

Mrs. McCarthy replied, "Well, then, slip him under the door. I'm in my bathrobe."

An Irish woman was visiting her sick aunt in New York. A week's visit stretched into a month. So one night she picked up the phone and called a male escort service. The manager said, "Madam, you can have your selection of male models, weight lifters, or male dancers—the most handsome and sexy men in the world. What would you like?"

The Irish woman said, "I'd like a guy about forty with a big pot belly, bad breath, and who's the worst lay in New York."

The manager said, "Madam, we have men who will fulfill your every desire. Why would you like a jerk like this?"

"Because," she said, "I'm not horny, I'm homesick."

A priest was walking down a Dublin street when he saw a girl in a halter top and miniskirt beckoning men from a corner. He went over and said, "Young lady. What would your darling mother say if she saw you on this corner?"

"She'd kill me," the hooker said. "This is her corner."

The Irish woman climbed on the bus with six children. She told the driver, "These two are thirteen, so they pay full fare. These two are eight, and they pay half fare. And these two are three, and they ride free."

The driver said, "Tell me, do you get twins every time?"

"No," the Irish woman replied. "Sometimes we don't get any at all."

How can you tell an Irish woman is ugly?
She even turns off her vibrator.

The guy walked into a bar and saw the Irishman downing double whiskeys one after another. He walked up and said, "What's wrong?"

The Irishman shook his head sadly and replied, "I gotta problem with my mother-in-law."

"Cheer up. Everybody has trouble with their mother-in-law."

The Irishman said, "Yeah, but not everybody gets her pregnant."

What's the difference between an Irishman and a Moslem?
An Irishman gets stoned before he sleeps with someone else's wife.

An Irishman walked into a bar and saw his cousin groaning as he downed a double whiskey. As the guy approached, he noticed his cousin had two black eyes and a big bandage covering his nose. The Irishman asked, "What happened to you?"

The cousin mumbled, "Seenus."

The Irishman was puzzled. "Don't you mean 'sinus'?"

The cousin said, "Nah. Last night I was screwing my next door neighbor and her husband seen us."

How can you tell your date's Irish?
When you check into your motel room, he puts a "Please Disturb" sign on the door.

Why was the Irishman so frustrated?
He finally woke up with an erection only to
discover both his hands were asleep.

How do you know your date's Irish?
His favorite sex aid is Fix-a-Flat.

How did the Irishman know he had a small penis?
His date asked him if she could use it to get out
a splinter.

⊘ SIGNET   (0451)

LAUGH 'TIL YOU CRY!

☐ **1,001 GREAT ONE-LINERS by Jeff Rovin.** The greatest one-line jokes, observations, and commentaries, for the first time, put together as a source of information and inspiration for anyone who wants to brighten up a conversation, a speech, or a piece of writing. Instantly prepare and swiftly serve up a feast of laughter.   (164229—$3.95)

☐ **THE OFFICIAL HANDBOOK OF PRACTICAL JOKES by Peter van der Linden.** A treasury of 144 rib-tickling tricks and leg-pulling pranks. This book will make your eyes water with laughter at the weirdest, wildest, most outrageously inventive and ingenious practical jokes ever assembled. Just make sure that when you read it, no one sees you doing it. Let them all learn about it the right way. The funny way. (158733—$3.50)

☐ **500 GREAT IRISH JOKES by Jay Allen.** Who are the nattiest men in Ireland? Find out the answer to this (and 499 more hilarious jokes)!
                                                           (168968—$3.50)

Prices slightly higher in Canada

_____

Buy them at your local bookstore or use this convenient coupon for ordering.

NEW AMERICAN LIBRARY
P.O. Box 999, Bergenfield, New Jersey 07621

Please send me the books I have checked above. I am enclosing $_____
(please add $1.00 to this order to cover postage and handling). Send check or money order—no cash or C.O.D.'s. Prices and numbers are subject to change without notice.

Name_____

Address_____

City _____ State _____ Zip Code _____
Allow 4-6 weeks for delivery.
This offer is subject to withdrawal without notice.